FEAR-
LESS-
NESS

FEAR-LESS-NESS

The Story of Lisa Andersen

By Nick Carroll

Preface by Lisa Andersen

CHRONICLE BOOKS
SAN FRANCISCO

PAGES 2—3: It was a treat to be photographed by Annie Leibovitz. I mean. she just shot a portrait of the Queen. Here I am at my home break in Ormond Beach.

PAGES 4—5: My first wave after being laid out for five days with a bad back.

Library of Congress Cataloging-in-Publication Data available.

ISBN-10: 0-8118-5481-7
ISBN-13: 978-0-8118-5481-8

Manufactured in China

Designed by Jacob T. Gardner
Typeset in *Adobe Caslon* and KNOCKOUT

Distributed in Canada by Raincoast Books
9050 Shaughnessy Street
Vancouver, British Columbia V6P 6E5

10 9 8 7 6 5 4 3 2 1

Chronicle Books LLC
680 Second Street
San Francisco, California 94107

www.chroniclebooks.com

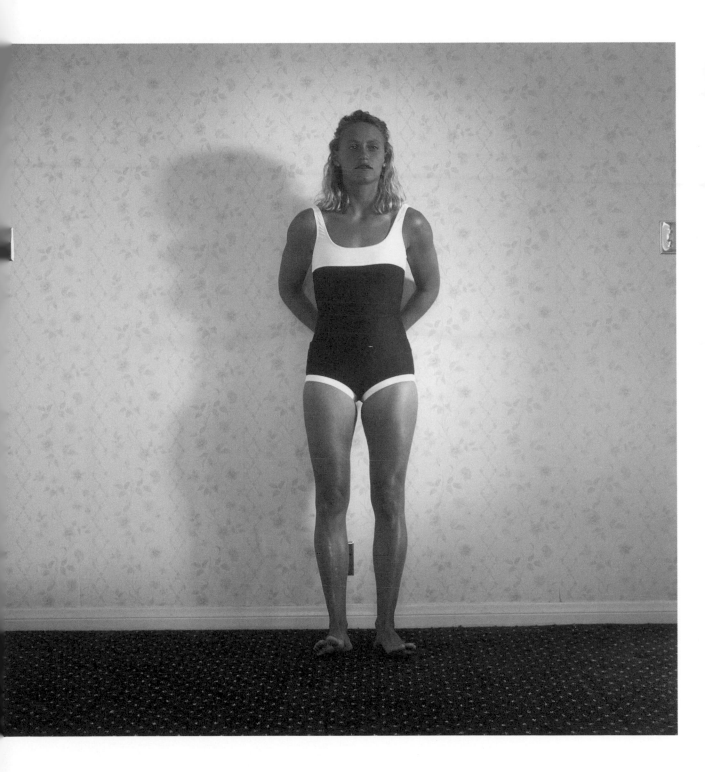

CONTENTS

PREFACE

By Lisa Andersen

It's six A.M., not that early for me. This is usually my favorite part of the day. It's kind of strange that I am writing this sitting in what was once my living room. It still smells like it used to, musty from the moisture outside. That's one thing I don't miss about living in Florida.

Having this book written about me has been a lot of hard work, emotionally—but it's also been an incredibly special experience, going back in time and reliving moments in my life, both painful and joyful. Overall it's been therapeutic and has given me an amazing sense of accomplishment.

I knew it was going to be tough to remember time lines, facts, names— but a lot that you forget comes back into memory once you start going through the details. Still, parts of this were much harder than I had expected, for sure. It was incredible compiling the photos, and I had a great time looking back into my personal history. Parts of my life that I'd never known about were revealed by my family—and I was educated about my family's background and history along the way.

It's been amazing, traveling the world, surfing so many great waves, experiencing victories and losses. Each and every relationship I've had, whether intimate or passing, competitive or friendly, has had an impact on my life and career. There were so many people who helped me make my dream come true. Winning that first world title was a mission. And doing it alone would have been impossible.

In hindsight, you want to go back in time and change things—do things better, with more strength or more knowledge. But had all of it not happened as it did, it would have changed the end result. The bottom line is, I was meant to be a mother first and a world champion second, and I would never change that!

One year ago I decided that I was ready for a career change. The idea of a comeback was long gone. And with both of my kids needing me to be home more, I had to cut back on travel. It has become harder for me to leave them, and so the reality had set in that I needed to start over, begin fresh. Funnily enough, I chose to move back to Huntington Beach, California. This time it wasn't running away.

With my relationship with Florida ending and my relationship with Quiksilver growing, I was given a great opportunity to still be a part of the sport of surfing. I am behind the scenes, almost. But I still travel to some big events on tour and get to see my friends. This is my chance to give back to surfing, the sport and lifestyle that has given me so much.

I love being a part of the industry right now. Eventually, I would like to move into having more of a personal life and take a step away from the industry side of the sport. I'd like to focus on bringing up my kids and getting back into my surfing, and to continue to discover new sides of surfing while it's still there for me.

It would be incredible to be surfing in the lineup with my kids one day. I have always wanted to share this love, to pass it down to my children. Neither of them has taken to it yet, but I didn't even start surfing until I was thirteen, so I don't rule this out!

I have new dreams now—not about winning world titles but about giving my kids everything I can. And, of course, the one in which I find great love that lasts forever.

Ormond Beach, Florida

INTRO-DUCTION

I'd known Ms. Lisa Andersen since she first began to travel on the world surfing tour, back in 1987. In early 2005, she sent me an e-mail. "I know you are busy with a current project but would you be interested in writing another book?" read the note. "About me of course."

Well, you know . . . *of course.*

Are you kidding? I thought. How could it be resisted? For a start, indeed, from the start, way back at the beginning of the twentieth century, the female presence in surfing has been profoundly unexamined. Perhaps even as late as 1987, for many male surfers, it was actually a source of some terror. How could women be *surfers*? The very notion challenged their idea of the sport, in ways they couldn't or wouldn't understand.

Today it's less revolutionary, and there are young surfer girls beginning to match boys turn for turn. But when Lisa first appeared on the surfing scene, that stuff was unheard of. To the high-strung boy pro surfers of the time, she was absolutely one of a kind: a girl who understood how to surf, from the inside. Here was a chance to see what all this—or even just a little bit of it—meant.

Besides, in any case, I just thought Lisa was splendid. That "About me of course" . . . I liked the dry wit, this woman amused by herself even in the act of requesting attention.

Yet Lisa was also a contradiction, and in the ensuing year, the more she and I talked, the more I saw how the contradictions flowed, even from the beginning of her story.

This was a woman for whom all sorts of things, in going wrong, had in fact gone right. She'd been torn away from a childhood home, only to be deposited on the Florida coast exactly where she needed to be, in order to learn to surf and to develop her incredible talent out of the limelight. She was coaxed into running away from that home, into a situation that could have ended in the worst possible fashion, but instead brought her into the almost immediate embrace of a wider surfing world. Then came her struggle with learning how to win . . . and how it delayed her success until precisely the historical moment when American girls decided they'd had enough of sitting around on the beach and wanted to do something in the water instead.

Then she became not merely a surfer, but something else. A legend? A brand leader? A lifestyle icon? It was just soooo freakin' *odd* . . . Lisa, a stubborn survivor, a single mom from Ormond Beach, Florida, suddenly the chosen leader of a girl-power generation! Like her world championships, it seemed in a way so natural, yet totally unexpected.

From other angles, the story looks like generational timing. Lisa comes from a family of strong women; if circumstances had been different, if the times or their lives had offered more opportunities, you wonder what her mother and aunts might have done. If Lisa's own surfing skills had emerged a generation earlier, they'd have done her almost no good whatsoever; the Title IX legislation that secured U.S. girls the right to take part in organized youth sports wasn't enacted until 1972, and organized professional surfing wasn't seriously under way until 1977. There was generational timing within the surfing world itself: for the first time, as Lisa began to win, a critical mass of baby-boomer surfers were parenting kids and ushering them—even the 51 percent who happened to be girls—into the waves. All sorts of events beyond Lisa's control or imagining had to play out just so in order to create the circumstances for her leap into legendhood.

In those lights, it's tempting to see Lisa's tale as Destiny—to let it fall into well-written cliché, to make her into history's tool. But nothing's that clear-cut, not if it involves human beings. While researching and writing this book, I found it hard at times to escape the oppressive sense of past events, the way they can hover over us and drive our actions, entangling us even when we think we're free as birds. I could see Lisa, with all her extraordinary strengths and successes, still struggling with how to see herself and her relationships clearly; still something in her in love with the chaos of her childhood. Still something in her, as Bruce Raymond told me, finding ordinary things hard.

But equally, you can't be sad around Lisa for long. Partly because she's a surfer, and to be a surfer in your heart and soul is to be happier than anyone else can quite believe; and partly because above all, Lisa does that grand and vital thing: she makes decisions. She makes them like she's swinging a sword, or a surfboard. She won't always know why, but she makes them, and sticks to them, and rides the consequences with what looks very much like fearlessness: the thought emblazoned on her gold necklace charm, the thought in the title of this book.

This is really why Lisa's story looks like an endless contradiction, and why in fact it isn't— because she's not just a tool of history, not just going with the flow, but an individual who sorts it out for herself, on her terms. And that makes all the difference.

—Nick Carroll, Oahu, Hawaii

PS: Something worth mentioning, by the way: Lisa's birthday, March 8, is the same as that of the legendary male surf pioneer of the 1920s, Tom Blake.

1. **TAKE**

A HOT SUNDAY IN MAY 1985, AND LISA ANDERSEN IS SIXTEEN YEARS OLD AND RUNNING AWAY FROM HOME AND HER FATHER ISN'T TRYING TO STOP HER.

Lisa has done everything. She's packed a bag full of clothes and a bag full of other stuff, photos, torn-out pictures from surf magazines, school yearbooks, memorabilia, teddy bears, everything but her birth certificate, which has mysteriously disappeared from the place she'd hidden it in case a chance like this came up. She's avoided a trip north to visit relatives with her mom Lorraine and her little brother Scotty, thus also avoiding the maternal pair of eyes and ears who'd have brought the whole scheme undone. She has $210 that she's sneaked out and withdrawn from the bank a couple of days ago, with nobody noticing, even though she is by the juvenile laws of the state of Florida not permitted to leave home without permission. She has a pillow for the plane ride she plans to take out of Orlando Airport, though she's never been on a plane in her life and has no idea how to book a flight, or even how much it might cost. She calls a cab, leaves a note under the other pillow on her bed, and tiptoes through the house with her bags and her pillow and her $210. Her father has been drinking in his living room armchair and now she thinks he's gone to sleep and she has no intention of disturbing his boozy slumber. Then the cab pulls up on the apron of the Andersen family home, pulls up in the shimmering rising

I was never there for picture day. This picture from Seabreeze Senior High's 1985 yearbook is the only high school class picture I have.

FEAR-LESS-NESS

heat waves of Bosarvey Drive, Ormond Beach, Florida, in late springtime, and the cabbie, with no idea of the thin hard drama playing itself out behind the house's drawn blinds, and hoping to get a response from whoever it is who's called, leans on the horn.

HOONNNNKKK!

Crap! What if he hears?

Lisa half-expects to see her dad come out the front door; he doesn't. If he comes to a window, sees anything at all, she doesn't notice. She jumps into the cab, tells the guy where to go, asks him how much it'll cost. Oh, 'round eighty-nine dollars, he tells her. What choice does she have? Christ, her stomach is churning, falling through her feet; she's scared to the edge of paranoia, and somewhere in there she knows what she's doing is bad, or might turn out that way. But she's going, she's gone, and she isn't turning back. Not for love or money or anything is she turning back.

"YOU KNOW, I WAS ALWAYS LOOKING FOR THE GOOD."

Lisa Andersen says this within five minutes of sitting down in her new office at Quiksilver headquarters, Huntington Beach, California. She plays with a computer screen, swinging it back and forth, taps on a keyboard. It's summertime, August 5, 2005, and she's recently been enlisted as global brand ambassador for Roxy,

the half-billion-dollar girls' surfwear label she's been endorsing since before the incredible girls' surfing boom of the past decade, the boom she helped bring about, the boom she's ridden like the biggest wave of her life. Lisa is even armed with her new business card. "Here, you can be the first to get one," she says, handing it over. On the card she's changed her title, to global brand representative. Surely it was ambassador on the press releases? "I wasn't comfortable with it," she says, but her boss, Randy Hild, doesn't know yet.

Classic Lisa: as she's done so often in her life, acting in secret yet in a way sure to be uncovered. Writing rules for herself.

"Mason!" she yells, good-naturedly, and her four-year-old son comes scampering out from behind a filing cabinet. "Mommy," he tells her, grinning, "I'm hungry."

Lisa sighs, grinning slightly herself, and swings her chair around and stands up in the same movement. At thirty-six years of age, she is loose enough, despite her chronic and potentially explosive back injury, an injury she's carried since before her first world professional surfing championship eleven years ago. She's very tanned, though she hasn't been surfing for a month.

She carries herself the way all great surfers do, arms loose, limbs straight and hanging from the joints, muscles toned yet not tensed. Nothing obvious, but every movement easy, free, and somehow unstaged. Her eyes are clear, sharp, and crystal blue.

You might not know it to look at her, but Lisa is a woman in transition. She's looking for the end to a journey she began twenty years ago, a journey she began with exactly the same move she's made this year—leaving the flatlands of Ormond Beach, Florida, for the flatlands of Huntington Beach, putting a nation between her and the fragments of a past she's yet to entirely understand. She's looking to leave it behind and start again . . . but how do you start a thing until you've finished what came first?

Sidewalk surfing with Mason. 2003.

FAMILY

ABOVE: *My brother Scott and me in Virginia.*
RIGHT: *Me in the high chair.*

Lisa Lorraine Andersen was born at 2:20 P.M. on March 8, 1969, in Brunswick General Hospital, Amityville, New York, weighing eight pounds six ounces, to John Andersen and Lorraine Andersen (née Scott). There were two half brothers, Edward and Duane, from an earlier relationship of Lorraine's. These are the bare details of her immediate family, a thin glimmer of the emotional world that Lisa entered, as far from the world surfing stage as she could possibly be.

Lorraine Scott met John Andersen this way: John was Danish by birth, divorced, and in the United States illegally, a merchant mariner who'd jumped ship in New York Harbor and was working for a Danish friend as a cook at a place called Tad's Steakhouse. When Lorraine first saw John, he was on crutches and nursing a new plate in his hip; he'd been injured in a car accident and was sharing a hospital room with Lorraine's best friend's father. Since John's divorce had left him with nowhere immediate to stay, Lorraine's best friend's mother invited him home.

With John, Lorraine was happy, for the first time in a while. Edward and Duane's father,

Eddie Senior, was long gone, and she knew her sons needed a father figure. It was some time before she figured out John might not be the ideal candidate for that task.

After Lisa's birth, they lived in Amityville on Long Island for two years, while John worked as a restaurant manager in a department store. In 1971 the store was sold, John lost his job, and at Lorraine's sisters' prompting, the family moved to Maryland, where he worked at an English pub–style restaurant called Ward Hardwick's before being transferred to another outlet in Virginia. There, from a traveling salesman, John and Lorraine heard about a job; a motel owner down near the small town of Fork Union, in Fluvanna County, Virginia, out in the boondocks some forty miles west of Richmond, needed someone to run the motel's restaurant.

They found a tiny house outside Fork Union, the former maids' quarters for an empty old mansion out in the woods: two bedrooms for two adults and three kids, with a tree growing right through the front porch. The Andersens, just another family swept up in the great American process—lifting up stakes and heading out, going where the work takes you, part of a nation constantly on the move.

The restaurant was a winner. Fork Union's biggest social feature is the Fork Union Military Academy, a boys' boarding prep school, and the Andersens had a captive market in the parents, who'd come down on weekends and take their academy sons out for dinner. And if there was one thing John Andersen knew how to do, it was run a restaurant. Lorraine used to marvel at his ability to handle food in quantity, his precise ordering, his lack of waste. They worked well together, John and Lorraine, each knowing what the other expected, each understanding the purpose of the work, each sliding into the kind of comfort zone that work can afford a married couple with a lot on their plates.

TOP: Mom and Dad. after they married.

BOTTOM: Those are my brothers Duane (left) and Eddie.

Time and work earned the Andersens a place in the local community, and the property one might expect to be attached to a solid and respectable family, with a profitable family business. In 1973 they bought a chunk of land a few miles out of town, eight and a half acres, and eventually built a proper family house on it, and so were freed from the tiny maids' quarters with its front-porch tree. In 1975 they were offered a lease on a restaurant space in the town itself, and since it sat twice the people, John decided it was worth the move. The restaurant was called the Wheelhouse; it had a seafarer motif and a seafood specialty, even up there in Fork Union, 150 miles from the ocean.

Success was theirs, or maybe it felt like success was teasing them—playing with them, the carrot and the stick. Back in Queens, Lorraine had been on welfare, after years of working as a supermarket cashier. Now she could almost picture it, the life she might soon lead, with the house and land and a white Cadillac to drive through town. Whatever the reasons, John and Lorraine worked harder than ever. They filled the Wheelhouse. They hired babysitters to cover the home front, and worked and worked, seven days a week, fourteen or more hours a day. Lisa can hardly recall seeing her mother at all during it, not for years.

Lorraine Andersen may not always have been there for her daughter. Yet women—powerful, determined, somewhat willful women—stand in the background throughout Lisa's family portrait.

At the age of six, Lisa paid a visit to her aunts Elaine and Edna, in Maryland. Edna and Elaine then drove her the two and a half hours back down to Virginia along State Route 15. Somewhere along the way, Edna, being of an imaginative turn of mind, began to make up stories to keep Lisa amused. "Look!" she said, pointing to the mounds of sand and gravel by the highway's shoulder, piled there by the authorities in case of an accident. "There's the White Cliffs of Dover! Do you know where they are, Lisa? They're in England! And look!" she said, pointing to a radio mast. "There's the Eiffel Tower, in France!" Edna kept it up, though she'd never traveled beyond the eastern United States in her life and never would, pointing out the wonders of the world to her small niece as they drove down Route 15 in 1975, and thirty years later, Lisa still remembers it clearly enough to say to Edna, last time they talked: "You know all those places you told

LEFT TO RIGHT: Aunt Elaine. Mom. and Aunt Edna.

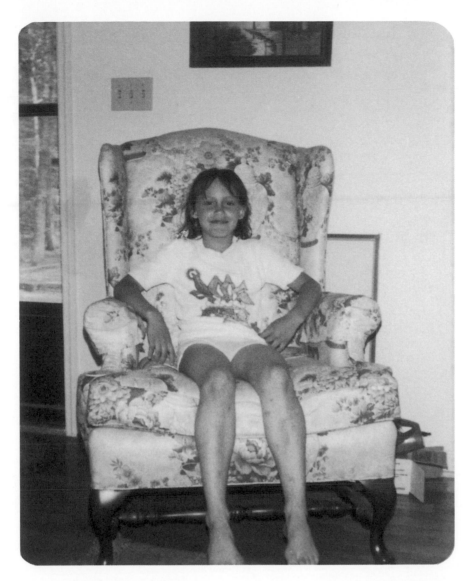

As a total tomboy in Virginia. I think I had just done something wrong.

me about on that drive? Aunt Edna, I've seen them *all*."

"I THINK THAT'S A CUTE STORY," says Edna. It's September 2005, a humid, saturating late-summer Florida Saturday, and she and Aunt Elaine and Lorraine Lemelin are sitting in chairs on the rim of the driveway at Lisa's house in Ormond Beach, overseeing a yard sale. "Damn! They're always doing this!" Lisa had scoffed, amused, back in Huntington Beach. "Wait till you see what they sell . . . just a bunch of crap!"

The three sisters sit in the driveway: Edna, tall and slim at eighty-two and intelligent; Elaine, larger, younger, fair-haired and fair-colored, and loving to talk; Lorraine, Lisa's mother, dark-skinned and gray-haired, energetic, and deaf. She recently settled on a cochlear implant, but she isn't satisfied with it. "I'm seventy," she says. "When I was nine months old, I was deaf in one ear from a mastoid growth. I think that's how I got good at lip-reading—I used to sit up front at school so I could watch the teacher speak."

Edna relates some family history. Lorraine has already recounted how Lisa is connected, through John, with the Danish storyteller Hans Christian Andersen. Now Edna says their forebears are Smiths, from England, through her mother Jeannette, though all these sisters are New York born and bred; even after decades of Ormond Beach, they all still crack a Noo Yawk whip on their vowels. Jeanette was divorced when Edna was three years old; as a result Edna was largely raised by her maternal grandmother. Later her mother remarried, to Silas Scott, a New York cab driver, and had five more children.

Lorraine grew up in this second family, in Jamaica, Queens. She'd inherited her father's coloring—dark hair and skin—and it flowed on down to Lisa. Lorraine respected her father, but she didn't think an awful lot of her mother. "My mother would take the household money and go to bingo and that used to piss me off, that she'd feed her children hot dogs so she could go to bingo," she says. "I used to think she was no kind of a mother."

My aunt Shane at my christening.

Another inheritance, emotional, generational: here are three women—Jeanette, her daughter Lorraine, and in turn Lorraine's daughter Lisa—all of whom have two lots of kids by two different men.

Elaine, both aunt and godmother to Lisa, is known in the family as Shane, a nickname she's had since childhood. It stems from the movie *Shane,* in particular the closing scene, in which the little boy calls to his hero, "Come back, Shane!" "That's what we were always doing," Edna explains, grinning. "She'd wander off into the distance and we'd be going, 'Come back, Shane!' She was actually being selfish. She'd go to the store and buy candy, and then walk off around the block by herself eating it so she didn't have to give us any."

Aunt Shane chortles behind her sunglasses. All three are wearing Roxy sunglasses.

None of the sisters really have a clue about Lisa's surfing. "We're all very proud of her," says Edna, "but where it comes from, we just don't know!" They're fascinated by a description of her skills, but still they evince no real understanding. Only later does Elaine reveal her own belief: "We're all into astrology," she says. "She's a Pisces. You know, she taught me how to swim when she was ten. Got me into a pool and taught me." She's still clearly affected by the experience.

"I mean the athletic ability was one thing, but out there in those waves, how could you not be scared?" says Aunt Edna. "It always amazed us that she seemed so fearless."

VIRGINIA FARM GIRL

Lisa herself didn't have any idea about surfing, in fact, not for almost all her first thirteen years. She wasn't a surfer; she was a Virginia farm girl who went to the beach at Cape Hatteras on short vacations, was allowed to go in the water up to her waist, and later couldn't recall having seen a single surfer, and that was it as far as the ocean went. In Fork Union, on summer days off, she roamed, wandered, packed a lunch and rambled through the woods on the Andersen property and beyond, crossing onto other pieces of land by ducking her head under a strand of wire. No fences. She'd follow millstreams all the way to the source, climb trees, eat mulberries in season, pretend she was having adventures, pretend she was running away, pretend whatever she liked. In hunting season she couldn't wander as far, and you could hear the sound of buckshot echoing through the hills, and her father, who loved hunting, would set tree blinds and go out in camouflage and try to get deer.

She had chickens and a couple of horses, but she was too young for that kind of responsibility, and the horses ran wild.

TOP: *My first catfish, which was too big for me to hold. 1973.*

ABOVE: *First vacation at the beach. North Carolina.*

My bedroom in Virginia.

**FEAR-
LESS-
NESS**

Vacation, North Carolina

She grew tall early, tall and skinny, like Lorraine had been. She learned to ride a bike, and would take it apart and try to put it back together differently, and build little jump ramps out of dirt in the driveway. Lisa saw herself as a tomboy, always in the company of boys. After all, she came from a family of boys. Her older brothers, Eddie and Duane, annoyed her in the way older brothers are supposed to annoy little sisters, and a couple of times they shot her in the leg with a BB gun. Her little brother, Scotty, had come along by then and he became a kind of accomplice of hers. Together, they learned to swim at the Fork Union Military Academy pool. Together, they set fire to the forest not far from their house. Lisa had a minor obsession with flicking matches into orbit, and one day the game got out of hand: a lit match flipped into a pile of straw, and it caught fire just like that, *whoosh*. Lisa and Scotty took off their jackets and tried to put it out, but all they did was encourage the flames. The fire began to build and climb into the forest. It was almost dusk. The children ran down the driveway toward their home. Their babysitter noticed nothing, not even when the big fire truck pulled up at the foot of the driveway, not even when the firemen came and knocked on the door. But word got back to John through the local sheriff, and that night Lisa was caught. You could go to jail for something like this, John told her, and he grounded her for a month.

Another afternoon, with another babysitter, Lisa and Scotty decided to go for a walk. They set off down the road, just the pair of them, and kept walking till they reached a friendly neighbor's house, around five miles away. By this time it was dark. *You sure you wouldn't like a ride home?* asked the neighbor, and they said, *Yes, please.* As they approached their home, they could see flashlights glittering in the woods. Closer still and they could see an ambulance, a fire truck, sheriff's cars. Half the town was out searching for the missing Andersen kids. The incident made the local paper, the *Rural Virginian*.

Not long after that, she decided she wanted to ride her bike the ten miles or so into town. So she just took off, swoosh, down the road, on her own, not telling a soul where she was going, a nine-year-old kid on a banana-seat bike riding along the highway, until somebody, a friend of the family, saw her riding around the military academy grounds. *Are you allowed to be around here all by yourself?* asked the friend. *Sure,* said Lisa. *Well, let's just take you over to the restaurant to see your mom and dad.* Okay, thought Lisa, I'm getting grounded again, yet feeling that little triumphant glimmer: *I did it.*

Stubborn Lisa, doing what she liked, taking the consequences, doing it again.

"I WAS TROUBLE WHEREVER I WENT."

Lisa is telling these stories while lolling around in a big chair in the front room of her new Huntington Beach abode, where her

Kindergarten

1st Grade

2nd Grade

3rd Grade

4th Grade

employer is paying the rent, just to get her settled in the first few months of her new job. It's late afternoon. Mason and his twelve-year-old half sister Erica are upstairs, by order of Mom. Lisa is curled half-sideways in the chair, one hand cupping her chin, face half-lit by sunlight reflected from the opposite wall.

"I wouldn't say we were troublemakers," she corrects herself. "I just took risks, went on adventures. I don't know if it was the getting into trouble I liked, or the thrill of actually pulling it off, you know what I mean? I obviously didn't care about getting punished. . . . Maybe I was looking for attention—who knows? My parents were never around. Maybe there's a lot there that explains it."

Have you thought about that since? "Yeah, I think about it. I'm just saying . . ." She laughs. "Should I lay on the couch right there? Like in *The Sopranos*?"

The phone rings. On the other end is Renato Hickel, Lisa's ex-husband and the father of Erica. Thus ensues a classic one-sided conversation as Lisa wanders off. "Where are you? . . . You're in Japan? . . . Oh, right, the Quiksilver Pro. Send me some money! Nah . . . but we've got to talk about it. She's an expensive girl, your daughter. . . . What, stay here?! Not in *my* room. I mean, you *can*, but upstairs, ha ha! No. Holiday Inn? Oh, of course, the contest is at Trestles."

She comes back, falls into her chair, sighs and groans at the same time. "Thank God for Renato. You don't get many of 'em. Just one, maybe."

In 1995, not long after Lisa's first world title, Renato went with her on her only trip back to Fork Union. The Andersens' first tiny house had vanished, seemingly into the forest. The Wheelhouse restaurant was still there, but its name had been changed, to the Wagon Wheel. Lisa was nonplussed by this brief step into the past. Fork Union was what she recalled, and it wasn't at all. "It seemed like a giant city then, to me, and now I saw there's one traffic light, and even it used to be a stop sign."

While Lisa talks, her face changes shape numerous times . . . or at least it *seems* to change shape. Lisa's is an extremely mobile face. In just a couple minutes of conversation it'll flicker all around, from innocent to contemplative to intense to charming . . . no, that's not the right way to describe it. Her face *actually seems to change*. The transformation goes beyond a mere

Cape Hatteras vacation. 1985.

tweaking of emotions, and it's not just the light. Lisa's had to present a lot of different faces to a lot of very different people, and when she's talking about the events of her life, particularly those at some remove, it's as if all those faces are shuffling through, mirroring the memories. A flicker of sixteen-year-old Lisa, trying to sleep in Orlando Airport. A flash of Lisa the mother. Lisa marrying. Lisa trying to ride ten miles into Fork Union, Virginia, on her bike. Lisa the loser. Lisa the winner. These chameleon shifts, they're part of what makes this conventional, almost ordinary-looking woman so extraordinary, so adaptable, such a . . . survivor.

Lorraine didn't want to notice John Andersen's drinking. She didn't want to see how John was with her two older sons. John had begun drinking fairly heavily soon after they'd been married, and after a while Lorraine began thinking, *What have I got myself into?* She worried about the future, about what might happen if she took some sort of action, where she and the children would end up. She watched as her husband worked endless days, drank, and descended at night into the fog of midlife. Sometimes he would be drunk and happy, sit there with that happy, silly drunk look on his face, and have Lisa sit on his knee and tell her that he loved her. *Yes, Daddy,* Lisa would say, *Enough, Daddy.* Other times he would just be angry at something the kids had done, and

he would uncork it in a surge of physical punishment, hitting the subjects of his rage with whatever was available: flyswatter, belt buckle, stick, broom, hand, foot.

Never Lorraine. Often Lisa. Always Lorraine's boys. John Andersen took his anger out on them with a vengeance. Eddie, the older, took it for a while, then he just split. At sixteen he left the household; at eighteen, right after high school graduation, he left town for Colorado and air force training. He never called or wrote again. He'll turn fifty in 2007 and Lorraine knows almost nothing of him.

Duane took it, though he was getting as much or more, having begun work in the restaurant after school. Lisa thinks Duane was made of stronger stuff. Duane worked for his money, bought himself a car, got responsible, bided his time.

Lisa took it, took the lot of it, crying and bruised, losing count of the wooden spoons her father broke on her. Sometimes as she grew older, she'd be beyond crying, and instead she'd go to that tough stubborn place she already knew inside and just laugh as the spoons broke, then have to run for it and be chased and hit again, learning nothing but pain.

A couple of times late in the Fork Union days, John's parents came over from Denmark. They were nice to Lisa and Scotty, yet something wasn't entirely right. John's mother was small and quiet, overshadowed by her large, hard husband. There was bad blood of a kind here between father and son; the last visit ended abruptly after they had an angry showdown, and John banned any future contact. Instead, unknown to him, they kept track of the grand-kids' progress through Elaine and her husband Frank—as, in a random sort of way, did Eddie. Aunt Shane, Lisa's godmother, became the conduit for her sister's fragmenting family life.

Lisa used to think, *I should be with Aunt Shane. I'm in the wrong family.*

In 1979 John decided to set up another side to the business—a fast-food take-out shop in a supermarket mall being built across the street from the restaurant. It was a barbecue place, selling everything from ribs and chicken to hamburgers, hot dogs, even mini-pizzas. It might not have worked even if the person John employed to take charge of it hadn't been robbing them blind. As it was, the destructive dynamic whirling through the family spread itself into the business, sucking capital out of the restaurant and away into the takeout's black hole. By the start of 1982, it was all gone, along with the eight and a half acres and Lorraine's dreams of a white Cadillac, gone into bankruptcy.

The mall owners offered Lorraine the restaurant to run; she refused, partly because she didn't want to emasculate John, partly because she didn't think she could do it. This left them unemployed, with little option but to move.

In February, scouting for restaurant jobs, John and Lorraine drove through Florida. They stopped in Jacksonville, which Lorraine didn't like, then came to Daytona Beach, where John got a job through an agency and stayed while Lorraine went back to Virginia to prepare for the move. On Good Friday, April 9, 1982, she and Duane and Lisa and Scott headed south with a packed truck.

Lisa felt utterly betrayed. Whatever else Fork Union was, this was the only home she'd known, and here were her parents forcing her to leave for reasons she didn't understand but instinctively distrusted. She'd been in Fork Union just long enough to receive a copy of the Fluvanna yearbook, for her seventh-grade year. She wrote a short, bitter note on the back page: "I didn't get this yearbook signed because I moved away. I hope someday someone will sign my yearbook."

Later she would look back and see the irony—this move she thought of as betrayal brought Lisa to the one place she could find within herself as pure a talent as has existed in the world of surfing.

AWAKENING

The only memory that I have of my dad at the beach. He didn't like us going in above our knees.

Picture where the Andersens pulled up after their drive down from Virginia. Picture Ormond Beach in summer: hot, humid, slow-moving clouds drifting overhead, cicadas shrieking in the trees. Not a lot of movement in the streets. The beach a long slight curve, the easterly rim of the great Floridian barrier island, lapped by warm lazy waters. Just south, in Daytona Beach, the buildings rise, painted in their childish colors, and people are beginning to pay their five dollars to drive out onto the pink-and-white sands in front of the crumbling old hot-rod hotels.

In between, a couple miles down from the Granada Boulevard inland route, lies Euclid Avenue—a dusty neighborhood, a little overgrown, rentals mostly, physically in Daytona Beach, though Lorraine swears the address always read Ormond Beach. You can picture in that fading afternoon Florida light, if you will, a thirteen-year-old girl with short hair, skateboarding down the white concrete of Euclid Avenue to State Road A1A, and a

Family life in Florida.

Here is what Lisa remembers from those first surfs at Ormond Beach off the Hartford Avenue approach. She remembers the first stages of learning to paddle, the phase of being so off balance that all your energy is spent just trying not to fall off the side of the board. Trying to sit up and balance on the board in the water and frustrated because she couldn't. She remembers many times trying to paddle out through all the whitewater and failing, or being swept down the long line of beach by the inshore drift and having to get out and walk back up and start again. Numerous times like that. Or making it out after three or four tries, catching a wave, and never making it back out again, and having to walk up the beach and wait for another try.

She remembers getting up and standing up riding the whitewash, taking off and falling off and being tangled up with people in communal wipeouts, heads over heels. She remembers catching waves and actually riding into the open face, and finally comes that one clear memory: of having stood up and turned into the face and driven another turn, a simple pumping turn but a turn done with control and intention along the line of the wave. There it is, the one memory. The connection. The imprint.

For a lifelong surfer, there is and always will be truly nothing like that first feeling of the wave, of being connected through and through in movement with the wave and the board. If you do this at a certain moment in your life, as

block north, to one of the little roads fronting the beach, Hartford Avenue.

This is Lisa's first surfing spot. The sloppy little wind waves she caught off Hartford, on boards borrowed from local kids she met at the foot of the concrete approach, slapped her awake to something entirely new.

Lisa did, when nothing else is quite working, everything in you will reset itself around that feeling. That feeling, in its absolute rightness, becomes the center of things.

When Lisa smells the scent of a certain brand of wax, even today, it hurls her back to those days of learning to surf, of hot days with the sand blowing along the beach, Florida sand so fine it dug itself into your wax and disappeared, only to scratch your tummy and knees when you paddled out. The thin Astrodeck grip pad near the tail, like the top surfers had. Eventually, a year or so into it, her first real board, all pink from tip to tail, the best thing she'd ever owned.

LATE AUGUST, 2005: LISA IS PERSUADED INTO THE FIRST SURF SHE'S HAD IN NEARLY TWO MONTHS.

She drives down toward Trestles, at the southernmost rim of Orange County, from Huntington Beach in her black Mercedes SUV. It's a classical hot, sunny, late-summer California day. "I feel like I've been turning into someone else," she says. "When I'm out of the water, my hair gets all greasy, I feel sticky . . . like a fish out of water."

Lisa prepares for the bike ride down the Trestles trail. She has two boards and doesn't really like either of them. All her nice boards are still back in the garage of her Ormond Beach house, awaiting transport to the West Coast. She picks a blue roundtail out of the Mercedes, holds it easily, looking down and across the board's center line, where the concave between the fins can be judged.

She wears a bikini top and bottom, a wetsuit vest, and a pair of shorts. In the surf, she says, "I'm trying to get 'em to cut these shorts back, shorter. Like, really short."

We are riding Lower Trestles on a slightly overhead south swell, and it's almost midday. Around forty-five surfers are in the water, forty of them men, mostly Lisa's age and older. They cluster on the outer peak, drawn to the chance of a larger set wave. "Men as apes," Lisa says, amused. "No matter who they are on land, they all do this in the water—try to get the biggest wave. Even if it turns into the biggest hassle."

The men all know she's among them, and begin to react, sneaking looks at this blonde casual woman cruising about halfway along the lineup. Is that her? That's Lisa? It's Lisa Andersen, it's her, Lisa's out here. Then a set of waves comes and catches them slightly unawares, and there's that characteristic minute and a half of intensity as everyone paddles, duck-dives, trying for one of the rights or lefts, trying to stay clear, riders leaping to their feet and lunging down the faces, waves rolling past.

Lisa lets it all go, waiting for an ice-breaker after her two months out and not wanting it to be a big show for everyone.

Foam climbing in the Turks and Caicos.

Now the few other girls in the lineup come over to her, shy but eager to talk. One, a thirteen-year-old freckle-faced gremmie named Courtney, is oddly proprietary; Courtney surfs Trestles a lot, and she wants Lisa to have a good time. "Go!" she yelps when Lisa paddles for a wave. Lisa chases a few, misses a few, silently grinning to herself at her lack of timing as the waves draw themselves away from under her. After ten minutes or so she finds one, a smallish right. She is easily to her feet, and despite the two months off, the blue board rises effortlessly into the falling lip of the wave, slashing out an arc of spray and driving down and away into another turn, then another, Lisa's face attentive yet half-smiling as she feels the muscle memory revived, the familiar pressure of board on water.

She surfs for a little less than two hours and comes in thinking she might be sunburned. "I get sooo burned here," she claims, talking about her first surfs at Lowers nearly twenty years before, when neon was all the rage and she wore a lime-green short john wetsuit, surfed for six hours, and burned her shoulders so badly she couldn't sleep for days.

On the trail back up to the freeway, Lisa's bike loses a nut and one pedal flops uselessly. A lifeguard is out surfing nearby; he notices, and practically falls over himself trying to help.

She rides up the trail, through the afternoon heat, her mind leaping back further now, to Ormond Beach. "I loved being out in the ocean," she says. "Once I got out there, I loved being out in the surf. Just accomplishing getting out there on the big-swell days when you'd see all your friends out there, screaming and yelling, in offshore waves. . . . It seemed like miles out when you finally made it, and it probably was. I guess there was so much of that pioneer adventurer in me who just liked to be away, far away from my parents and school. Even though I wasn't supposed to be in there, I didn't really do it to piss my parents off. I loved the feeling of being in the ocean. And that part of it, that they didn't approve of it or like it or wanna be a part of it, made it that much harder of a thing to do. I still don't understand it."

Once upon a time, Lisa used to dream of surfing with her dad. She's had dreams that Lorraine's out surfing with her, out paddling around with her on a longboard—Lorraine, who doesn't

After a good one.

even like getting wet under the shower. Perhaps she dreamed these things because that was the only place they'd ever happen, in her dreams.

By now they were calling her "Trouble" down at the Hartford approach—first because she'd endlessly pester them for a turn on their boards, then because she was soon enough moving faster than anyone her age, taking waves from all over the place.

Not that the local boys, guys like Dave Hettle and Ronnie Hope, minded Lisa hassling them. They responded to her the way many surfers would to the flood of Lisa-inspired girls who'd hit the waves over a decade later—with encouragement. They'd hoot and holler Lisa into waves, coax her into them, tell her to paddle hard! Go for it! This little all-male surfing bubble-world felt to Lisa like something she instinctively knew, Lisa the tomboy who'd

PAGES 38–39: *This is the first surf shot ever taken of me. I still stick out my chin when I surf.*

grown up in the company of boys. It felt as it has to generations of surfers on beaches from Ormond to Waikiki: a kind of family, yet free of an actual flesh-and-blood family's weird demands, its unbreakable ties and inexplicable undertows.

Plus surfing fed her increasing need for rebellion. Here is how Lisa described it, years later, to a Brazilian TV station: "I started surfing right after my parents told me I couldn't do it."

To Lorraine, surfers were what she'd seen in Tab Hunter movies: drunk beach bums, bearded and sleeping on the sand. To Lisa it was as much about style: Vans checkered skate shoes, Levi's, Op walk shorts, Sundek baggies, the stuff she'd see in magazines, or in the Salty Dog surf shop at Bellair Plaza, just north of Hartford. The style of kids like John Logan, one of the hottest surfers in town and the coolest kid in school. Johnny was small for his age—driving his first car, he had to sit on phone books—but he had a blond mullet, and girlfriends, and he was sponsored. Just to surf! Amazing.

She surfed, and then she did every small infuriating thing she wasn't supposed to do. She stole change from her parents' room and bought cigarettes, then she stole cigarettes. She plumped up her bed with pillows at night and sneaked out to skate around Bellair Plaza till two A.M., when Lorraine would get a phone call from some other baffled parent and have to go chase her down. She met a kid who lived nearby, and they would just not go to school; they'd walk around and find somewhere to hide, then head to the beach, which got her picked up by the police on more than one occasion. She toyed with drink, played with drugs, mainly marijuana; the couple of times Lorraine found some tucked away in Lisa's room, Lisa just sneaked into her parents' room and repossessed it. Well, she figured, they're not gonna use it.

She flirted with boys, kissed a few, becoming sexually aware, but not letting anything go further, not yet.

There were parties, drink, and drugs, but there was surf, surf, always surf. . . . And Lisa got one wish, at least. Her copy of the Seabreeze Senior High School yearbook of 1984–85 has signatures throughout it. The book leaks the optimism of a beachside city in the age of Ronald Reagan. "Our World Is Constantly Changing—Nothing Stays the Same," reads the opening headline. The Class of '85's motto is this: "Never regret the things you have done, Only the things you have never tried."

Plenty of schoolmates have written little messages, most addressing Lisa as "Trouble" or "Troub." There's a range of views on this unknown quantity, this future superstar of Seabreeze High's coolest sport. Mariana says: "Can you believe you actually survived your first year at Seabreeze! You're the sweetest girl I know— you're so crazy too! You better be good over the summer, and don't get in TROUBLE!" A warier note is struck by Carlene, who writes: "I'm glad that we have been able to become friends. You're super sweet, except at certain parties. Since that disagreement is over with, I hope to see you

next year." "Troub, it's been fun having you in Human Dev. I'm sure I'll see you on the beach. Have a great summer. Love, Albert. PS: Surfers Rule!" Faculty editor Joyce Hayes wants to join Trouble in the water and "shred the waves together."

There's no photo of Lisa on the Surf Club page. There's a photo of a goofyfoot named Tina Selden; above the photo Lisa has written tersely, "Can't surf." Lisa's photo is farther along, in the Clubs section. Lisa, blonde, boyish, curling her lip at the camera yet somehow vulnerable, set apart from her peers, the only one in her club: "Troub Club."

"Now that this year's over and we're juniors we're gonna rage!" writes Glenda, leaving her number. "I know I'll see you at the beach." But she doesn't see Lisa at the beach. Lisa never graduated from Seabreeze High. By the time graduation came around she was gone.

REAL
TROUBLE

Mom. Scott. and me. 1986.

It is an afternoon in early 1985, in the Andersens' living room, and Lisa can't even remember what she's done this time. Skipped school again? Sneaked out the window? It was wrong, whatever it was, she knows that. Dad is facing her down, Mom next to him, both of them reprimanding her, and for the life of her she can't recall why. Lisa looks around the room, seeing the familiar things: Dad's chair where he always sits, TV in front of that, kitchen opposite, and back to Dad, who is beginning now to rant. Angrier and angrier. Goddamn it! he shouts, turning red, his voice beginning to trip over the words in his thick Danish accent, thick enough so she can't clearly hear what he's saying. Maybe he's even speaking Danish by now, swearing at her in a tongue she doesn't understand. I'll show you what you get, he says, and is out of the room and back again in a moment, now holding the Board, Lisa's all-pink surfboard, her prize possession, her connection to whatever it is she's found out there in the waters off Ormond Beach.

You want this, here's what you get.

John drops the board down flat on the floor, and then he does something that none of the three will forget. He jumps on it. He jumps on it over and over, square on the tail, so the fins break and the fin box mounts are driven back up through the brittle foam core and almost clear out through the deck. He jumps on it and it is smashed, irreparable, ruined.

Lisa watches, feeling removed, dissociated, as if it's happening in slow motion. She'll think of something smart-ass to say in a moment, she's sure of that, maybe something like, "I can always get another," though she knows that's not likely to happen. But while her father breaks her board in front of her, for those slow-motion seconds she can't think of anything at all.

Lisa was in deeper waters than her schoolmates knew. The Andersen family was disintegrating. By this time they'd moved again, from Euclid Street to the more salubrious Bosarvey Drive, closer to the center of Ormond Beach. It was their last throw of the dice, their last courting of financial and familial success. Lorraine was awake to John's alcoholism now, no longer inclined to give it shelter, and presented him with the options: divorce or treatment through Alcoholics Anonymous. John attended AA for a week, then came home and told Lorraine, They've got the problems, not me. Lorraine pushed Lisa to attend Al-Anon family support groups. Lisa, contemptuous and afraid, thought it was a joke.

She looked for new ways to rebel and found one: Ray.

Ray Ferrantelli. Twenty-four years old. Parents owned a grocery store in Ormond Beach. Ray was short, strongly built, a competent surfer who made surfboards with a couple of the local kids, and talked of being a great boardmaker, of living in Hawaii, of climbing surfing's Everest of skill. Ray locked on to Lisa, skinny dark-skinned surf girl Lisa, whose home was collapsing around her. Ray was wary of Lisa's father; John had caught Ray and Lisa hanging out together once and threatened him with a shotgun. He didn't dare come to the door of the house; instead she'd sneak out and around the block to surf with him.

In early 1985, Ray left Florida and ended up in Huntington Beach, working in a surfboard glassing and production shop, writing Lisa letters about his new life out there in Surf City. Sending money. Sending the rice-paper surfboard decals from the companies whose boards he was glassing. Come out and join me, you're unhappy there, come out, here's the money, come. Ray's siren song.

Lashing around for attention, thinking already about running away, she borrowed a friend's moped bike and disappeared for a day and a half. The friend reported his moped stolen, Lisa was found and arrested and taken to the Volusia County Juvenile Detention Center, charged with grand theft. In the past, when the cops had picked her up for truancy, Lorraine and John always went dutifully to collect their errant daughter; *this time,* Lorraine thought, *I'll leave her there. Maybe she'll learn a lesson.*

Lisa was in the Juvenile Detention Center for nine days and learned nothing other than that it was full of kids worse than her and that her parents had left her there. At the end of the nine days she appeared in court and was released into their custody on the condition of restricted movement. Home, school, court appearances, and juvenile counseling sessions, always accompanied by a parent; otherwise nothing.

They sent a counselor to the house to try to talk to her. Stubborn Lisa would go to her room, shut the door, put on the record player and turn it up, drowning out the attempt to communicate.

By May, Lisa's life was splitting in two. She saw the two futures before her, the two she could imagine, anyway: one the house restriction and juvenile detention and family dissolving around her; the other unknown and frightening and free. One hot Sunday, with nobody to stop her, she made the choice.

Lorraine headed home from Maryland the following week, getting stuck at Exit 4, four hours north of home, when the car broke down. She called John to see if he could help out somehow. He couldn't, he said.

Where's Lisa? she asked.

She's gone.

What do you mean, she's gone?

She left yesterday.

Lorraine couldn't comprehend what he was saying. And where were you? she asked.

I was sitting here in the living room.

She cursed him from then on.

Once home, she found the note under the spare pillow in Lisa's room. Later Lorraine would throw the note away, deciding she didn't need the bad memory, but what she recalled it saying was: *I'm not a bad person. I did not commit a crime and I will not be treated like this. I'm leaving and I'm going to be the number one surfer in the world.*

My bedroom in Florida. The photos pinned up on the wall are
of Shaun Thompson. Barton Lynch. and . . . Dave Parmenter.

2. THE WIDE, WIDE

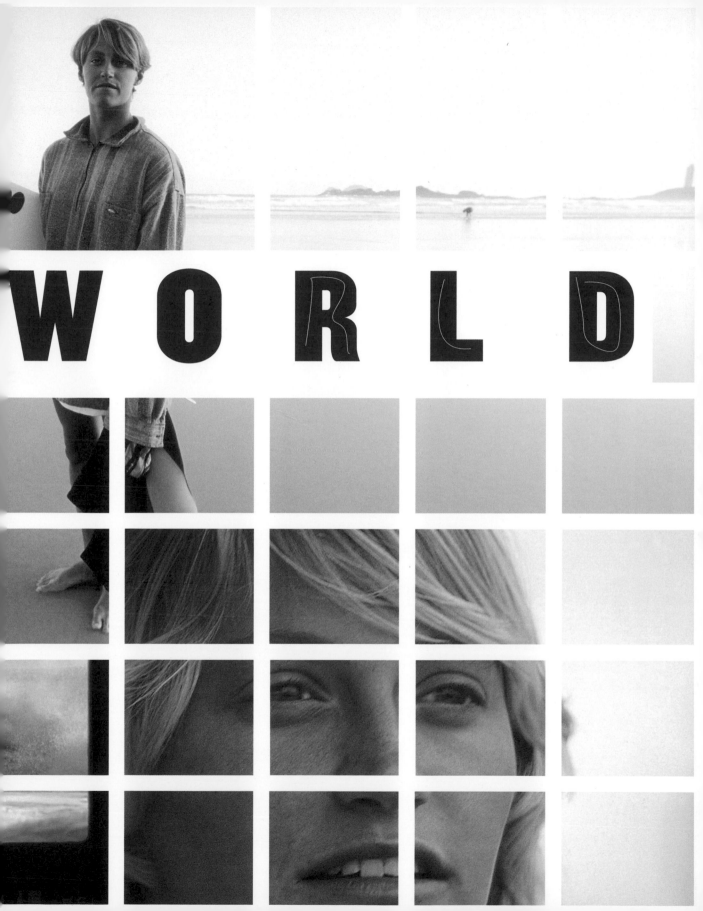

WORLD

$\mathcal{L}$ISA WOULD SAY LATER SHE DIDN'T KNOW WHAT SHE WAS WRITING IN THAT NOTE, THAT SHE DIDN'T EVEN KNOW THERE WAS SUCH A THING AS A WORLD SURFING CHAMPION. This is odd in a way, since the 1985 women's world pro surfing champion was the shy yet ruthlessly skilled Frieda Zamba, a resident of Flagler Beach, Florida, barely twenty miles north of Ormond Beach.

In another way it wasn't odd at all, because you could count Frieda's appearances in the surf magazines of the day on one hand. If there were girls in the magazines in 1985, they were usually wearing bikinis, and they surely didn't surf.

But oh yes, there was a surfing world out there, bigger than a kid from Florida could imagine. What was Lisa getting into? In 1985 there were over two million surfers on the planet, all of them owing their engagement with the waves to an ancient Polynesian practice, half sport, half ritual, a game the Hawaiians had called *he'e nalu,* or "wave sliding," a pastime almost lost toward the end of the last century before its revival at the hands and feet of the Hawaiian princess Beatrice Kaiulani and a relaxed and motley bunch of Waikiki waterboys. Surfing had arrived at Huntington Beach almost at the start of the new century, thanks to a rail baron who hired Irish-Hawaiian surfer George Freeth to put on a promotional display of surf-riding.

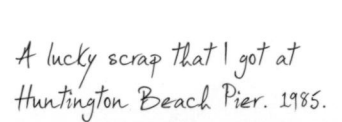

A lucky scrap that I got at Huntington Beach Pier. 1985.

FEAR-LESS-NESS

In time the sport had spread across the lower coasts of the Golden State, in the process becoming part of the great Californian romance. Surfing was part of a postcard being mailed back to the rest of America. "Wish you were here," read the postcard, in among photos of palm trees and the Hollywood sign and the Beach Boys, "the water's fine!"

Yet it was nothing like that, either. Surfing was—surfing is—hard. Becoming good, really good, at it was not far from impossible. You did it on freezing winter mornings when you were colder than you'd ever been in your life; you did it in an ocean that sometimes seemed very likely to drown you; you did it surrounded by fast-moving hostile people who wanted your waves and would take 'em if they could, by stealth, skill, trickery, or outright aggression. Shot through with mythology, wanderlust, adrenaline, competitive energy, and fear-born respect for nature's power to kill or thrill or both, surfing wasn't a postcard at all. It wasn't even a lifestyle. It was a Life.

None of it was real to sixteen-year-old Lisa, not yet. To her, fresh off the plane from Orlando, sitting in a car beside short, dark Ray Ferrantelli and still emotionally rattled from her getaway act, L.A. was as it's appeared to countless bewildered travelers on the West Coast migratory passage: on-ramps and off-ramps, twisted and mangled concrete highways all entwined, mountains of cars

and roads, horizon blurred by smog and rising heat. Then driving off the 405 freeway and out to Bolsa Chica just north of Huntington Beach, she saw a beautiful sunset, almost dark, the sun strangely positioned on the ocean horizon, so it felt like morning to Lisa's East Coast mind. And she saw the waves . . . small waves, but lines of waves like you'd never see in Ormond Beach, Pacific Ocean lines rolling in past the oil rigs far offshore and breaking on that long straight beach.

LISA, SEPTEMBER 2005: Lisa walks across the train tracks at San Clemente Pier, out onto the pier itself, sits on the deck at the Fisherman's Bar, and orders an espresso. She's on her way to San Diego for the Action Sports Retailer trade show; this is what she does now, this is the job of a global brand ambassador. Small waves crumble next to the pier, where she surfed once with John Parmenter, her once-boyfriend Dave's brother. "John was soo rude! All the time. Dave used to say, 'Surf with him at your own risk.'"

She laughs. She is wearing big dark sunglasses. A small inscribed gold plaque hangs around her neck on a thin chain; in small letters stamped into the gold it reads

FEARLESSNESS.

Just how big a step Lisa made in May 1985 is difficult to imagine until you discover she'd been in two—only and exactly two—surfing contests before deciding to back herself, to go with her intuition, by running away to Huntington Beach. To put it into context, this is a little like doing a couple of school plays then going to Hollywood in pursuit of an Academy Award—with the idea you *could*. "I didn't have a very long amateur career," she says. "Went to the world contest in England in 1986. Still wish I'd won that. Then I won the Katin at Huntington—the only time it had a women's division. But I was amateur, so I had to give the prize money to Alisa Schwartzstein, who came second. Then I did another one, one of the PSAA events, and won that, and had to give the money away again. I started thinking, Why shouldn't I go pro?"

Competitive surfing at the peak level is a kind of addiction. Lisa's trying to let it go, but knows she hasn't, not completely. People ask her to surf in World Championship Tour events as a wild card, but she always says no, even when part of her wants the opposite. She may not have moved on yet, not yet have become the person who can go to trade shows with perfect ease and a sense of corporate mission, but she knows enough not to prolong that addiction. "It just hurts too much . . . when I lose 'cause I'm not in rhythm, 'cause I don't surf enough heats. I'm not a good competitor."

Lisa never was a good competitor, not in the strict sense of focusing everything on defeating an opponent. What she always did—and does—is surf, using such spectacular natural gifts that they override any thought of surfing being something "only boys do."

Lisa understands surfing, the core of it, the inner sensations and how they relate to the outer performance, with the kind of casual, intimate

My bottom turn throughout the years.

confidence you see in few surfers and no other females. She describes a good day in mid-2005, back home in Florida: "I had three sessions. The first one I was just fooling around, messing up, getting out the stiff parts. Then the next one started coming together. . . . The third surf I could see the whole wave before I even stood up. One of those surfs where every turn is better than the last one.

"I'm my own worst critic. A hand out of place and I'm worrying about it." How does she *know* a hand is out of place? She sidesteps this question.

Curren was the style model—Tom Curren, the Californian champion of the 1980s, whom many aficionados think of as the finest pure surfer ever. "Ian Cairns and Tom had this video series they did. Years ago. I'd love to see it again. It was of Tom in small waves at Trigg"—in Perth, Western Australia—"and there's a part where it's just shots of Tom's feet on the board, riding along these little waves. And you can see it so closely, toe to heel to toe, ankles, knees . . ."

She rolls her hands in the air, demonstrating the easy, rail-to-rail flow that was always Tom Curren's hallmark and can still be seen today, albeit incompletely, in almost every champion surfer's approach. The hands, too, matter to Lisa as they did to Curren—the stroking of the wave face in bottom turns, the arms held up almost in surrender as the board is sent high

into the lip. Almost dreamily, she says, "You can see it all the way out to the fingertips."

What did Ray see in the teenage runaway he'd lured across a continent? Maybe Ray Ferrantelli was just the first of the men who could see the greatness in Lisa, that part of her just beginning to awaken to the wide, wide world. Maybe he thought she could be controlled. If so, he was mistaken. Ray was renting an upper-floor apartment back along Huntington Beach's old Main Street, and glassing surfboards at Spanner's glass shop, where Huntington's big names, like Carl Hayward and Robert August, had their surfboards laminated. Downstairs were the classic surf shops, Jack's, George's, their dark-stained walls lined with surfboards and memories.

Ray had one bed, a mattress on the floor in his apartment. Not seeing much option, Lisa slept on it. Things happened on the mattress at night, things for which Lisa didn't give her permission, things she tried to shut out of her mind even as they happened. Where else would she go? She was a sixteen-year-old runaway; she'd made her choice and she hadn't seen the next choice, not yet. She pretended to be dead, or somewhere else, while Ray did what he wanted.

To get out of the apartment, she'd spend the whole day in her wetsuit at the beach, dawn to dusk, riding the board Ray had given her, a Randy Rarick Surfboards Hawaii design. She learned to fine-sand boards in Spanner's for a few bucks, found a part-time job at a frozen yogurt store, then moved on to waitressing at Mizzardi's, an Italian restaurant on the highway. Lisa the restaurant manager's daughter, doing what she knew, busing tables. Nights she'd crawl out of the apartment window and sit on the roof of the building next door, listen to music on a little tape player she'd found, and look down on the glory of Main Street before its glossy modern rebirth—dirty old Main Street of Huntington's grand old tough days, with the punk bar across the street and the people fighting outside, and the cops coming down to break it up.

After a few weeks of this Lisa found out about a surf contest coming up at Southside Huntington, run by some organization she didn't know, the NSSA. The day of the contest, a Saturday, she was up long before light, getting out of that apartment, walking down the sand under the deadening gray blanket of June-gloom Southern California fog, looking for the good.

Ian Cairns found her there, curled up half asleep under a judging table, an hour or so later when he came down to begin the process of setting up yet another event. Cairns was a surfing legend of the old macho school, a huge man from Busselton in West Australia who'd made his reputation in Hawaii, winning contests at places like Haleiwa and Sunset Beach. In 1981, Cairns had his last year on tour; he was living in Huntington Beach, trying to build a surf business with fellow Australian émigré Peter Townend, when they were offered positions as executive directors of the National Scholastic Surfing Association,

Surfing out to the fingertips in Indo. 2005.

an amateur surfing organization founded in 1978 by Huntington Beach's Chuck Allen. The NSSA's focus was clean, straight-up competition in a wide range of divisions, tempered by an educational requirement; it was home for an emerging generation of Southern Californian surf kids, clean-cut and studious.

Ian saw his NSSA as a family-driven operation, run on the beach by him and his then-wife Pat, something solid for a loose surfer to lean on. Under Cairns and Townend, the kids got fifteen-minute heats, started from the beach, under any conditions; the best four waves scored, and there were contests in your local area twice a month. "We had the idea that it might be hard, but fair," Cairns says today. "No debates over judging, you had your chance to go out and do your best, you took it or you didn't."

Anyway, by 1985, their events were honed—sponsors, systems, and status, lent by team member Scott Farnsworth's 1984 world contest win and the huge success of NSSA alumni Tom Curren and Mike Parsons. As Ian says, "It was a logical place for someone to show up with aspirations. . . . She knew what she was after."

Cairns figured, this girl is distressed and alone, we should make her feel welcome. Thinking he was providing a sort of charity, he gave her a start, despite Lisa's lack of a local school record or a parental signature. Watching the heat, he realized he was involved in something other than charity: "It's not often you turn over a rock and find a diamond."

Lisa was paranoid all the time, thinking the cops would pick her up, discover she was a runaway with a Florida juvenile record. The truth was she didn't stand out much . . . just another surf grom in Surf City, running down the street with board and wetsuit, hanging out at the surf shops. With her short hair and drowned-rat post-surf look, you might not have even picked her out as a girl; and anyway, what girls surfed?

Somewhere in there she was busted for jaywalking, and a cop wrote her a ticket. After a while, when the ticket wasn't paid, a notice was sent to Bosarvey Drive, Ormond Beach. This is how Lorraine discovered where her daughter had gone—a jaywalking notice from the City of Huntington Beach. However stressed she'd been in the months beforehand, she'd always figured no news was good news. Now she had news, but was it good or bad? She recalled Ray's name, called the operator, got a phone number, and dialed that number. A man she guessed was Ray answered. *Where's Lisa?* she asked.

One minute, he said, then: *There's nobody here by that name.*

I know she's there with you, said Lorraine, *and if she's not with you, you know where she is. You tell her from me that she can call anytime. The past is the past. The door's always open.*

Not long afterward, Lisa called.

Here's how she got away from Ray Ferrantelli: she left and never went back. Well, not quite.

FEAR-LESS-NESS

My first studio session with Art Brewer sometime in the late '80s.

The apartment block was growing fouler by the week. Homeless people. A shared bathroom down the hall. Lisa was gaining traction now; she knew people, good people, Cairns, Shane Stoneman, Mark Caffey, other kids from the NSSA. Hey, only the other day she'd been riding her bike along Pacific Coast Highway, and Craig Comen, team manager for Aleeda Wetsuits, had come out of Aleeda's front door, stopped her, and offered her a sponsorship! Four free wetsuits a year! And yet here she was, stuck in this place with this guy she feared and distrusted, faking every minute.

She took every excuse she could to stay away. She'd sleep at Stoneman's, Comen's, anywhere she could. The days away from Ray added up to weeks. In this floating, semidetached life, Lisa met a girl who lived with her parents off Main Street, a smart high school girl named Heidi, and for a month or so the pair hung out a lot. They walked Lisa's bicycle down Main Street one afternoon, turned the corner where the street bends away from the beach, not far from the apartment, and there in front of them was Ray.

He was on a bicycle, too, and he rode directly at the two girls and ran square into Lisa, knocked her down, began hitting her, yelling, When are you coming back? Where the hell have you been? Get your ass back to the apartment! Heidi was scre aming and he was swatting at her too. Partly to defuse the situation, Lisa began walking her bike toward the apartment block. Ray went in first while she held the door, then he came back for her bike and took it to walk up the apartment stairs, and Lisa just let the door swing shut and ran, Heidi next to her, saying What's going on? Wait! Ray chasing them all the way, two blocks up Main Street and off onto Heidi's street and under the half-closed garage door of Heidi's house.

There they all found Heidi's father, and for the second time in his association with Lisa, Ray found himself looking down a parent's gun barrel. Get your ass outta here, buddy. Ray got his ass out.

Lisa didn't leave the house for five days, until Heidi's parents saw she wasn't shaken up anymore and told her it was time to move on. That happened to Lisa often around this time in her life, as she wandered on and off the couches of friends and acquaintances: Sorry, the parents would say, but you can't stay. We don't want any trouble.

"Trouble," Lisa laughs, twenty years later. "I had the right nickname."

She walked out of their house at the end of those five days and Ray was one of the first people she saw. He was hanging around the corner of Main Street, waiting for her. He told her he was sorry and she could pick up her stuff anytime she liked. Which she did.

Now Lisa became a wanderer, homeless, sleeping anywhere she could, lying to friends and parents to get another night on a safe couch, and when that didn't work anymore, sleeping next to her board on the beach. In the mornings she'd go to work at the yogurt store, using the staff bathroom to clean up. One night, desperate, she remembered a friend down at Newport Beach who'd gone away on a family vacation, so she climbed into the house through a window off the upstairs deck and slept in the living room.

Yeah, it was frightening . . . but it was incredible. Huntington Beach! At the surf shops, during the big summer pro contests, the wide world came to her and introduced itself. She would go down to the biggest contest of them all, the Op Pro, and look through the plastic mesh fence at the surfers, great surfers; Brad Gerlach, Shaun Tomson, Tom Curren, Cheyne Horan—they'd all be in there waxing their boards and talking about heats. Then one morning, one of them says to her, *How's it going?* Cheyne, it was, the muscular grinning blond Australian.

Good, Lisa says, *I'm good*. They talk for a minute or two, then out of nowhere, Cheyne asks, *Wanna go surfing? Want to go down to Trestles?*

Lisa says, *Yeah, sure! Where's Trestles?*

You've never been down there? Cheyne's amused. He has a little VW Beetle, with the front seat bent back so you can load in the boards; Lisa sits in the rear like a good grom should.

They drive down the freeway to San Clemente, and Cheyne says, I gotta stop at a friend's house to work out first, do you work out?

No, says Lisa. They pull over to a house near T Street in San Clemente, where Cheyne's buddy has a garage full of workout gear, and she hangs out and watches Cheyne lift weights for a while, thinking *This must be what real pro surfers do.* Then they're running down the trail toward Trestles, Cheyne in his bright orange wetsuit with his purple keel-finned board, Lisa with her new bright pink wetsuit from Aleeda. And they're bumping into Jimmy Hogan, the fiery Californian, and his friend, the already legendary Martin Potter, who are on the way down, too, for a photo session with the big *Surfing* magazine photographer Larry Moore. Everyone is there, and here is Lisa, first time at Trestles and going surfing with Cheyne Horan.

She skins her knees on the rocks and doesn't care one bit.

Another time, she meets another Australian, Kingsley Looker. Kingsley is taking a girl she knows from one of the Main Street surf shops to an Eagles concert in Irvine, and Kingsley's friend Brian Heritage is going too and doesn't have anyone to take. So Kingsley and Brian invite Lisa along. She's sixteen years old and going to a big rock concert with a couple of pro surfers, no strings attached. After the concert they just drive her back down to Huntington and drop her off near the beach, saying, All right, grom, see ya later.

And she was developing as a surfer. Lisa approached the crowd at Huntington Beach Pier with contained aggression, her talent overriding the boys and men in the water around her. She was hungry for it, chasing anything, any kind of competition she could find. If there wasn't a contest at Huntington, Lisa would get in the car with Craig Comen, Stoneman, Caffey, maybe Todd Miller from Newport Beach, and they'd take off, driving down to San Diego, up past the Ventura County line, sometimes all the way to Santa Cruz to the nearest NSSA or Western Surfing Association event, and spend the weekend surfing. On Sunday night, totally fried, they'd get back in the car, Lisa with her first-place trophy and everyone else with whatever they'd managed to pull, and drive back to Huntington, where they'd eat pizza and go to the movies. Usually to ones Craig liked. Lisa saw a lot of Clint Eastwoods, a lot of Arnold Schwarzeneggers.

Life slowly stabilized. She got to know Tricia Gill, a pro surfer from Newport, and Tricia introduced her to her aunt, the 1982 world champion Debbie Beacham, and Lisa ended up staying for a while at Debbie's house while Tricia and Debbie did the tour. She walked the dog, cleaned the dishes . . . an odd little interlude. Debbie took her to a surf-industry trade show at Long Beach and tried to find her some more sponsors. She also introduced Lisa to a coach named Glenn O. Kirkby, who decided Lisa needed Hawaii experience and just sent her there, out of the blue, for a week in March 1986.

She surfed Rocky Point and came back not a lot the wiser.

Eventually she moved into Greg Mungall's apartment in Costa Mesa with Comen, who'd become her boyfriend. Craig Comen in his early twenties was powerful, curly-haired, fired up, a skilled surfer who'd done some travel time trying to make a name for himself on the world pro tour, found his limits, and turned to the then almost unknown job of corporate surf-team manager. Through him Lisa met the George brothers, Sam and Matt, and world tour pro Dave Parmenter, whom Comen knew from his years of living on the Central Coast. She and Comen got into coaching, crazy stuff nobody else was doing. Video sessions, for instance. Aleeda owned this primitive old video camera setup, just a big box-looking thing with wires and leads hanging out of it, and Craig would lug it down the sand and shoot hours of tape. Not even sure what they were doing, they'd go back to Mungall's and analyze and critique their surfing, in total passionate surf-nut mode.

"I don't know if she had a goal," says Comen, today. "She was just so competitive. She wanted to beat people, to be the best she could. Maybe as a distraction from other things, but it became more than that." Craig had a short fuse himself, but Lisa cracked him up, the way she'd take on boys in the water, paddle them down, and get more waves than anyone. Once, they were surfing Newport Beach, around 36th Street, and Comen looked around and saw these two guys walking away fast along the beach with their boards, and sure enough, Lisa chasing after them, all by herself, furious, letting 'em have it over some indiscretion or other. No average dork was getting the better of *her*.

Yet still she seemed vulnerable, younger, more innocent than any sixteen-year-old runaway had a right to be. The movie-buff George brothers called her "Newt," after the little girl in the movie *Aliens*, who Ripley finds hiding in the air-conditioning system—the girl who looks frail, but who survives. The girl who finds a way.

Ian Cairns had a longer vision. Ian had surfed with and known the awesome women surfers of the 1970s, that spectacular first modern generation, who by Lisa's time had already passed into myth: Jericho Poppler, Rell Sunn, Anella Sunn, Lynne Boyer, Linda Davoli, Margo Oberg. "They had *mana*," says Cairns, using the Polynesian term for life force. "I was just a kid when I met them, at the 1970 world contest, and I thought they were much more impressive human beings than the men. The Roxy girls of today are a teenybopper version of that."

He says he hoped Lisa might become something like that—but more so, because she surfed better. These men, one after another, projecting their hopes and dreams onto Lisa Lorraine Andersen, the runaway from Ormond Beach! No wonder, as she grew into this male-dominated world, she chose her mates carefully, for what they could provide.

I think this was taken at
J-Bay. I'm still in awe of
that wave.

LISA, SEPTEMBER 2005: Sometimes there is a sense of Lisa as very solid, very knowing, and you're aware instantly just how far she's come from that vulnerable runaway. As she sits one afternoon with Renato in her house in Huntington, Lisa laughs and tells about a recent phone experience: "My dad was on the phone and he was sooo drunk, I couldn't really understand what he was saying. . . . He started crying, saying he was sorry and all that. Then there was a call-waiting, I told Dad I couldn't talk right now, took the other call, and it was you!" She points at Renato. "Then while we were talking, I got another call-waiting—it was Dad, again!"

She chuckles drily. "All you'd need was for Dave Parmenter to call and you'd have the whole thing right there." Renato gazes at her from under his eyebrows, in good-humored reproof.

THE REAL THING

To Lisa, she and Craig Comen weren't a big boyfriend-girlfriend kind of deal. To her, Craig was support, surfing buddy, coach, boyfriend—kind of in that order. To her, it wasn't exactly forever, and maybe it started coming undone during the World Amateur Championships at Newquay, England.

This was late fall 1986, and Lisa, along with Janice Aragon, had made the U.S. team, and she had a lot of fear in her about the opposition—girls she'd never surfed against before from places like France and Tahiti, and the powerful Australian Connie Nixon, who everyone seemed sure would win. It did her head in to think about it, and the more she thought about it, the more she felt like she was already losing. Give Lisa time at a surf contest to think about things and she'd wander off down all sorts

of blind alleys, half the time bringing her natural talent down around her ears. She'd think about anything but what was in front of her. In Newquay, on her first trip away from American soil, she made the final and paddled out thinking about Craig on the beach, telling her what to do and which waves to catch, and something in her—stubborn Lisa, doing what she liked, paying the price—just clicked off. Running third,

with a shot at the title, she began to paddle in and away from the lineup. *There's no waves out here anyway,* she thought. Comen was talking to her from the sand, in normal tones at first, then yelling: *Get back out there! Catch a wave! Just catch a wave!* Lisa was filled with her stubborn, fuck-you energy. *No!* she thought, ignoring him. Whereupon Craig, frustrated out of his mind, started picking up small rocks, pebbles really, and throwing them at this maddening girl who wasn't doing what he'd told her to do, what he *knew* was the right thing to do . . .

By this time Lisa had outgrown the NSSA, and Comen always knew she'd outgrow him, too. "She was young, she had a taste of freedom and wanted to fly. The success was coming and she was just starting to taste it." He sounds a little sad, saying it, even twenty years later: "I knew she was going somewhere and I didn't wanna get in her way."

Dave Parmenter was the real thing, a fully fledged professional surfer and one of the finest America had ever produced, ranked in the Association of Surfing Professionals' top twenty, indeed one of the best surfers on earth. Blond, blue-eyed, squarely built, Parmenter was nevertheless the precise opposite of the California surfer-stoner stereotype; fiercely intelligent, not inclined to easy friendships yet intensely loyal to his friends, he'd moved from his mother's Newport Beach house way up into central California's

Dave took me to a beach that had Kangaroos on it.

cold-water country, where he trained, designed surfboards, wrote magazine articles, and lived the avid life of a total surfer, as far from the postcard version as he could get.

Lisa didn't think much of him at first, considering him standoffish and arrogant, but he grew on her over time. Like with the autograph he gave her. There's an old saying in surfing's boys-only world, one that's mostly been erased with time: "Boards and broads don't mix." When Dave wrote an autograph for Lisa, she found he'd rewritten it: "Boards and broads DO mix."

Hmmm, she thought, *maybe I've cracked this guy.*

Lisa got to know him better in 1987, her world-tour rookie year. She'd arrived in the Australian city of Newcastle in October, pretty much clueless. That was Lisa in those days, a couple of years older than the runaway from Ormond Beach, but still willing to roll the dice on a trip to somewhere she'd never been. She found herself sleeping on the floor of a hotel room above a pub, sharing with a couple of Aussie juniors, Craig "Scat" Pitchers and Jason Buttenshaw, and Jason's dad. Secondhand smoke was drifting up between the floorboards. Lisa went looking and found Parmenter and his friends Mike Burness and Greg Anderson, knocked on their hotel room door, and they took her in. They couldn't believe she'd chosen this tough steelworkers' town, Newcastle, for her first visit to Australia. When they all lost early in the contest, Greg said, Okay, I'm gonna take you guys down to Sydney to stay at my place, and we'll go

surfing down there, you've got to see it. So they did, drove the two hours south to Sydney and roamed its northern beaches, surfed the famous Narrabeen beachbreak and the other beautiful spots up and down the stretch. Just another traveler's memory, another thing Lisa doesn't always remember yet won't ever forget.

A couple of months later, early in the new year, Lisa and Craig drove up the Californian coast toward Santa Cruz for a contest there, planning on doing some surfing along the way. Parmenter's place at San Luis Obispo was a natural stop. The current of feeling between Lisa and Dave got Comen upset; he left early, raced up the coast, and got in a fight in Santa Cruz. Lisa stayed behind and drove up with Dave the next day under a blue sky along that wild coast near Big Sur, butterflies flittering in her stomach. After the contest she went with Dave to his place on the Central Coast, and she never went back to Huntington . . . not for decades.

"But hey," says Lisa today, "I thought this was the real thing. A big deal. Kind of that first-love thing, for sure." Within a few weeks she and Parmenter were traveling together, to Australia again, spending two perfect weeks on the rural coast south of Sydney with Tom Curren and his wife Marie, playing couples, camping out, watching movies, surfing. Kind of that first-love thing, for sure.

In San Luis Obispo they lived in a small house on a big piece of land: two little bedrooms, a living room, and a kitchen. The sun

Billabong grom way before Roxy.

went down behind the house at an angle each day. The property's owner had given Parmenter permission to build a surfboard-shaping room, which Dave turned into two rooms, one for shaping, the other just a surf-dedicated room, with boards and pictures.

Parmenter's intellect awed her, perhaps even frightened her, eventually bored her. Occasionally she felt so illiterate, she almost didn't dare get into conversation with him. When Sam and Matt George were there and they and Dave got going on some amazing strand of surf history or philosophy, the Virginia farm girl would have no idea what the hell they were talking about. She couldn't interrupt him while he was reading. At breakfast Dave would have a cup of coffee and a magazine, not a newspaper, and he'd read it and could not be disturbed. Eventually Lisa decided to let him educate her; she asked him for lists of words he thought she should know. He'd write out five or six at a time and give the list to her, and she'd go off and dig up their meanings and learn them by heart.

The surfing they did blew Lisa's mind. It was so incredibly unlike the days at the Hartford Approach in Daytona, where you could run down the street and be in warm water in five minutes. On the windy, open coast near San Luis Obispo, they'd drive for an hour before they had a clear idea of the conditions, sometimes three or four hours before they'd decided where to surf. Sometimes it would be all Lisa; she has hours of videotape of herself surfing the beachbreaks at places like Pismo Pier, while Dave carries on an endless hilarious commentary, in which Lisa is kicking the asses of all the surfers he hates on tour . . . "Whaddya think about *that* call, Al?"

FEAR-
LESS-
NESS

Other times, they'd pull over in the middle of nowhere, walk across some huge cow pasture, clamber down a cliff, and paddle out to something that barely resembled a wave, and it would be so cold and sharky that Lisa would be over it in forty minutes, back up on the cliff, trying to warm up. Dave would stay out for hours.

"I'd sit there and watch him and think, 'He's nuts,'" she says. "But in a way I dug it too. Like, he's crazy, but I like it."

Now Lisa's world grew wider still, and not just through Dave Parmenter.

In 1987 and 1988, the ASP world professional women's surfing tour was a scrawny add-on, a sideshow in a male-dominated, male-run sport. It boasted nine events and just over $83,000 in prize money. Lisa had barely enough support from various sponsors—Billabong, Rip Curl, and a few others—to get to eight of 'em. In Europe she slept on the floor of an apartment rented by John Shimooka and Rod Kerr, two of the tour's most relentless partyers, and was only saved by fellow tour rookie Sunny Garcia. Sunny, the big loose Hawaiian with the unfathomable streak of anger, had a soft spot for Lisa. "I don't know what it was, maybe we had similar backgrounds, both trying to get away from our parents," he says today. "But we connected, and I made sure she wasn't too hassled by all the boys on tour who were trying to move in on her." Sunny was always a sucker for a vulnerable girl.

Still she had her share of fun with them, like the quick fling with rising Australian star

Brazil. 1989.

FEAR-
LESS-
NESS

Gary Green, whom she baffled in a moment of passion by looking into his eyes and asking, "Can I borrow your six-six tomorrow?" Greeny was stunned. "It's like going surfing with your mate and then going home and chocking 'em," he told *Tracks* surf magazine.

Pretty soon half the men's tour was secretly in love with Lisa, even if they couldn't quite figure out why. Lisa was good-looking, but it wasn't just that. She *liked* boys. She didn't mind their company the way some other pro girls seemed to. Heck, half the time the girls looked terrified of the male pros, with their casual swagger, their boyhood arrogance, their ferocious speed and skill in the water. The men wore their contempt for the women pros' skill level on their sleeves, openly and unthinkingly, but they didn't scare Lisa at all. When Shmoo or another of the boys gave her cheek, she'd smile her special Lisa smile—wicked one moment, warm the next—and give it right back.

She surfed better than some of them, and well enough to earn their respect. They could see she had that inner understanding of the wave, all the way out to the fingertips. Her surfing, her wicked wit, her fearlessness eroded the tour's vast gender barrier. She was a sister in a brotherhood.

She established a results pattern: she'd breeze through the opening trials rounds, then be booted out of the main event pretty much straightaway by one of the top girls: Frieda Zamba, or the talented Wendy Botha, or ultraexperienced Australian Pam Burridge. Lisa had entered an arena where her natural skills weren't quite enough—or so it seemed, in the presence of these girls, with their tactical sharpness, their ability to choose a wave and block an opponent. She would lose heats to aggressive paddlers like Alisa Schwartzstein just because Alisa or another pro would force the issue, racing for waves, and Lisa would be flustered by the aggression and just let 'em go. Then afterward Lisa would get an attitude over it, the sneer of a talented rider beaten by tactics, protecting herself emotionally from the loss: *I'm a better surfer, so who cares?* When she lost that way, the boys would come up later and boost her ego: Who cares? they'd tell her. She was the better surfer anyway; the other girls were all kooks.

Then she would say things about the girls' tour, how she was keeping her distance because she'd heard there was a big gay scene. "I'd heard they were all lesbians," she told *Surfing* magazine a year or so later, aware by then that she'd overreacted. "Most of the heavy girls who were really into it and showed it, they don't really do the tour anymore." Tricia Gill, Lisa's brief benefactor from Newport Beach, hit back with a tart letter to the magazine: "It's a sad statement that she prejudices her opinions and actions towards these people with a form of bigotry. This is the '90s and there is no need for her continued rudeness and fears."

The straight-shooting Aussie Jodie Cooper has since told her she was a cocky little shit at the time, something Lisa believes now, though she never wanted to be that way. "But I had all the guys on my side," Lisa says today. "I had more of the guys respecting me than the girls who were the best in the world. And I had to go with my ego a little bit."

She was disappointed by Frieda. Here was the world champion from a beach a half-hour drive north of Ormond, and Lisa could barely get a hello from her. Frieda Zamba and her soon-to-be-husband, Flea Shaw, were a self-contained unit on tour, and Frieda didn't go out of her way to be friendly with any of her competitors, but Lisa took it personally—or took it as a guide, of sorts. She decided that if she was ever to be the champ, she'd try to stay outgoing, friendly, down-to-earth. Being popular mattered to her, and on tour it seemed she was popular for the first time in her life. Did

winning mean you'd be unpopular? Should she even try?

Wendy Botha was different. Lisa befriended Wendy almost as soon as they'd met, at the Op contest in Huntington back in 1986, when towheaded Lisa had asked her about a million questions. Of all the women professional surfers, Wendy was closest to Lisa, in some interesting ways. Both were feisty, stubborn, blue-eyed, blonde girls who surfed hard and got along well with boys. "We used to perv on guys a lot," Wendy says with a grin today. "We had that in common."

Wendy grew up surfing Nahoon Reef in South Africa, and while she'd had a happier home life, her surfing experience had been very much like Lisa's. While learning to surf, she'd been one of the boys, aware they were looking

after her all the time. She had a six-mile walk from her home to the beach, and guys would turn their cars around on the road to give her rides there or back. She traveled with the boys on tour, too, and still remembers driving twelve hundred miles to Bells Beach from Queensland, Australia, with Martin Potter after Pottz had won a HiAce truck at the Queensland Stubbies contest—despite the fact that neither of them had a driver's license.

That first year of Lisa's, 1987, Wendy smashed her way toward her first world championship, unseating Frieda Zamba with the best all-round professional act the women's tour had seen. She'd show up at the beach with her trainer and her manager and stretch out in front of everyone, as if to say, *See, I've got a whole team behind me, and I'm coming to kick your ass!* Lisa hung out with Wendy; they were friends, even though Wendy was beating her in the second round at almost every event.

If some of the women were unimpressed by Lisa's cockiness, Wendy decided Lisa was just speaking her mind, a quality Wendy liked. "Plus I felt for her," Wendy says. "She'd had a hard time growing up and she was always battling something.

"I used to think, Oh dear, she's as good as me—then I began to realize she was *better.* I knew it would take her a long time to get all the pieces into place, but that if she ever got it all together we were all gone. Once someone like that gets some confidence, you're stuffed. Then she'd have a brain explosion in a heat, do

something ridiculous, and we'd all sigh with relief.

"She'd freak out and tell me, 'I'm never going to win!' I'd say, 'Man, you're the best surfer, it'll happen for you.'"

Still, Wendy was disinclined to actually make it happen for Lisa. For quite a while she held the upstart at arm's length, telling her, "You'll have your time, but right now it's my time, I'm gonna beat you, so get stuffed! Wait in line!"

In 1990, Lisa won her first big tour event. It was the Bundaberg Rum Surfmasters, of all things a competition sponsored by a giant distillery, at Burleigh Heads. Lisa made the final and faced Pam Burridge, and won when Pam couldn't make her last score count. High on it, she drove south to Bells Beach with Dave and won there too, in a performance the former world champion Damien Hardman would later call "the best I've ever seen a chick surf—ever." Oh those boys, with their backhanded compliments.

Back then things were so loosey-goosey that after the day's proceedings, the pro events would give you the prize money right there and then, often in cash. The surfers would line up at the door of some little office at the event and shuffle in and be handed this big roll of bills by Al Hunt or whoever the tour manager

Biarritz. 1990.

happened to be, and that was that. Lisa took over $20,000 in cash away from the Australian events. In May 1990, five years after she'd climbed frightened into a cab outside a blind-drawn house in Ormond Beach, she and Dave flew home to San Luis Obispo and she went straight downtown and bought a new TV, a stereo, a VCR, a collection of movies, and a new Super Nintendo computer game machine. They set the whole lot up in the ranch house and got into crazy Nintendo battles and watched movies all day between surfs. Heaven.

By now, happily, Dave and Lisa were engaged to be married. By now, painfully, she'd ended a pregnancy. The one moment as romantic as they could make it, the other as dismal and sad. She wasn't ready for a child, and Dave definitely wasn't. A child of divorced parents who hadn't spoken to his own father for years, he saw parenthood through a glass, darkly. "It was not the right time and both of us knew that," she says today. "It was traumatic because there were medical issues, and I don't think we ever talked about it. I was so scared, man."

Lisa is in the kitchen of the Huntington house, speaking these words over a half-empty cup of coffee, gazing down at the counter. It's impossible to tell what she's thinking.

Meanwhile, Dave was becoming increasingly disillusioned by the tour. In 1988, as he, Lisa, and the Currens were on their way back to the big Coca-Cola Surfabout contest in Sydney from those perfect weeks on the New

South Wales south coast, he discovered he'd missed a crucial heat, and his tour seeding had bounced back to thirty-one—out of automatic entry to big tour events. Dave became a savage and spectacularly witty critic of pro surfing. Later in the year he rode a longboard for one wave in a heat at the Op Pro, mocking what he later called, in *Surfing* magazine, "the glove-wearing, bathroom-slippered, traction-decked, over-ornamented wags who are making a mockery of what was once a simple and beautiful thing." The judging panel scored him 2.5 out of 10 for the ride.

Soon afterward Matt George published an interview with Dave in *Surfer* magazine, under the title "Iconoclast Now," quoting his satiric vision of pro surfing's future: "Come one, come all, to the Greatest Show on Earth! With the fat lady, the sword swallower, and JoJo the Russian dog-faced boy!" As Lisa's surfing hero Martin Potter smashed his way to one of the biggest world-title routs in pro history, as their friend Tom Curren came back from a year's break to win his third world championship from absolute scratch, Dave set more and more borders around his surfing life, refusing now to drive farther south than Santa Barbara in search of surf. Lisa listened as he criticized even Curren, said Curren was a kook for taking this thing seriously. The tour, having cast him aside, was now something he despised.

It tormented Lisa to hear this, to see it. She loved him, and she loved his surfing—no matter what, she thought that part of him was magical. But she hated how he'd turned against the thing she wanted so badly. For by now, two or three years into it, Lisa was hopelessly caught up in the tour. Already she'd invested in it with all the instinctive stubborn hopeful energy she possessed. The childhood among boys, the running away, the lonely wandering in Huntington, the half-formed bits and pieces of a life on her terms—this was unconscious training for the one task her sublime surfing skills fit like a glove. She fit like a glove. Out there, on the road, she was a runaway among runaways; they were eternal runaways, all of them, together, brilliantly talented hoboes, wandering around in their traveling circus in celebration of precisely what Lisa had discovered within herself.

No way was she letting that go. Not then, not yet, maybe never.

Early in 1991, she made one of her silent secret instinctive decisions. She told Dave she was going down south to check out a contest in San Diego, asked him for a ride to the border at Santa Barbara. She hitched a ride from there with the young pro Chris Brown, and ended up on the couch at a friend's house in San Clemente. Lisa had heard a buzz that Quiksilver, the fastest-growing company in the sport, might be on the lookout for a woman pro, that Wendy and maybe Pauline Menczer were putting together résumés. She quit her then-deal with Op, who hadn't paid her for months anyway, and called Quiksilver's Bruce Raymond and pleaded with him for a ticket to the next tour stop.

She—her decision—broke Parmenter's heart. Brutally, finally, completely. He was still calling her, sending flowers, still trying to figure it out months later, by which time she'd landed for the first time on the Raymond family's doorstep, a whole ocean away in Avalon Beach, Australia.

Mugging in a little black dress.

STROKES OF FORTUNE

Lisa, the Virginia farm girl turned Ormond Beach runaway turned unlikely surf star, got to Avalon Beach and she never went back. Not for years.

Janice Raymond, used to surf grommets landing on her doorstep, opened the door to this scruffy kid straight off the plane with short blonde hair and a surfboard bag, and thought she was a boy. "Hi, mate!" she said, "what's your name?"

Lisa opened her mouth and said, "Lisa." *Ohhhh-kay,* thought Janice, *this'll be interesting.*

Bruce and Janice and their family were the stroke of monumental fortune Lisa needed: Bruce, the former top-sixteen pro surfer now in the driver's seat for Quiksilver's international team; Janice, the warm, straight-to-the-point woman with whom Lisa immediately clicked, the sister she'd never had.

"She was a full-on tomboy," says Janice today. "There wasn't a feminine thing about the girl." These days the Raymonds live in a kind of impossibly beautiful house facing into Pittwater, an estuary inside Sydney's northern beaches. The house is wide open to the winter sun and gorgeously furnished, a symbol perhaps of these amazing times, when surf companies are worth

TOP: *Being goofy in Australia. early '90s.*
ABOVE: *Bruce Raymond with his sons Nick and Ben.*

billions and even runaways earn money they'd never imagined. . . . Yet in a little room off to one side, where Janice and Bruce are sitting and nursing cups of tea, there's a reminder of other days, an old wooden table they call the Truth Table. Because when you sit there, says Bruce, "It's where the bullshit stops."

The Truth Table's seen a lot of talk, a lot of tea, and a lot of Lisa. It's why Lisa still likes to make tea not with a bag but in a pot, with loose tea leaves, in the old Australian and British manner. It was the centerpiece of the Raymond family kitchen in their old, far more modest home in Avalon, the house where Lisa first knocked on the door back in 1991.

Bruce and Janice lean on the Truth Table and talk about what struck them about the girl on the doorstep. "Just how comfortable she was, her poise," says Bruce, meaning her surfing. "Most female surfers have an awkwardness about 'em, it's not ugly, but they have a little bit of an awkward style and approach. But the thing that stands out about Lisa is there's none of that. She's a natural. She doesn't have a style as such, she's just a natural. Her poise. We hadn't seen that before."

Janice watched with great interest and some amusement as her houseguest morphed over several months from some cool little surf chick to a complex weaver of tangled female webs. Parmenter would call and she'd say, "I'm over it!" and refuse to take the phone. Meanwhile, she'd met young Avalon pro surfer Graham Wilson, who'd come around and look at Lisa with what Janice thought of as "puppy dog eyes." Perhaps partly because Janice had recently lost a sister almost Lisa's age and look, the two grew close very quickly. "That was the thing about Lisa and me, it was straight up," Janice says. "Because she'd never had a mother she felt she could tell anything to, no sisters, a scattered family, dysfunctional, I was just like, 'Oh you can tell me everything, I don't give a shit, I'll tell you everything.' She knew she could tell me, there wasn't anything she could shock me with. And I'm not old enough to be her mom."

Lisa loved to take photographs, and Jeff Hornbaker had turned into one of her better friends on tour. Hornbaker, a tall piratical near-hippie of a man, originally from California and now based in Hawaii, was one of the surf world's finest photographers. He'd been one of the people to tip Bruce off about this original girl surfer, so different from the other female pros of the time. He and Lisa got hold of some Quiksilver gear, took it down to Avalon Beach, and did a shoot. The resulting photos wandered the Quiksilver offices, an odd intimation of what was to come: a girl looking vulnerable and cute and strong in clothes made for boys.

These were all men's wetsuits. in the pre-Roxy days. Australia was the only market willing to advertise to women.

FEAR-LESS-NESS

Lisa went to Japan in May, competed, and came back to Avalon, pretty sure she was going to stay here forever. On Sydney's northern beaches, she could surf most days with Pottz, Wendy, and the legendary Australian champion Tom Carroll. Surfers weren't runaways in this big coastal town; instead they were praised as sporting heroes and interviewed for TV shows.

Jeff Hornbaker — my inspiration.

Maybe, to her, it seemed a kind of ideal version of Florida, Ormond Beach the way it should've been: an estuary waterway, a long peninsula of land, a series of smooth thick-grained sand beaches broken by rocky headlands. The sun rose over the ocean; the waves were short, choppy, coming all in a rush; you could ride fifty, seventy, a hundred in a session. Lisa surfed, talked Bruce or anyone she could into shooting

video, watched it, surfed some more, growing into herself and her skills.

Around the time Lisa was getting to know the Raymonds, Bob McKnight was trying to decide what to do about Roxy.

The 1980s had seen surfing's second big modern boom time. Boom Number One, in the early 1960s, had been all about numbers in the water, as the new lightweight foam and fiberglass surfboards gave surfing to the masses. Number Two was less about people and more about money: crazy Reagan-era optimism, building a consumer wave that helped surfwear labels like Op, Quiksilver, Billabong, Body Glove, and their cousins grow almost out of hand. By the decade's end, surfing wasn't a cottage industry anymore; it was the Industry.

Half-formed niches began developing in this mad young market, and McKnight, the man in Quiksilver's hot seat, began to plan for them. In 1989, he and his marketing director Danny Kwock thought about starting a women's line. They figured they should begin in the water, which at the time meant one thing: bikinis. (BIKINIS! BIKINIS! BIKINIS! read the deathless cover line on *Surfing* magazine's 1989 Swimsuit Issue.) They hired a designer and wondered about a name. Quik Femme? Roxy? This from Kwock, who'd liked the word from the moment he'd seen it on the marquee at L.A.'s Roxy Theater; he thought it sounded stylish yet a little punk, a little edgy. Both McKnight and Quiksilver cofounder Alan Green had

daughters by that name, and McKnight says he was a little against it for that very reason, yet Roxy became a working title while they searched for something else.

Meanwhile, a swimwear line was developed using the name. By spring 1990, they had some pieces ready to show at the September trade shows that year, and did, with some success.

In 1991, Boom Number Two's bubble burst. Surf clothing companies, energetic but naive, had bet the farm on 1980s styles rolling over into the new decade more or less untouched. Instead they got their first serious lesson at the hands of the market. Those neon trunks and blow-dried shirts came back from the surf shops and department stores in piles.

Boom-time budgets weren't ready for this. McKnight, facing a 30 percent decline in his major market, had to make some hard decisions, cutting back on all the bits and pieces, all the minor labels gathered around the Quiksilver logo in pursuit of those nebulous niches. Roxy, the budding swimwear ranger, closed.

But it didn't die. Mel Matsui, who worked on Quiksilver's successful denim line QSD, kept putting the Roxy label on the short shorts and the little denim dresses . . . not out of any strategic mission, but because Mel liked the look.

In late 1992, the recession having been part of life for over a year, the Quik crew had a sales meeting on Oahu's North Shore. There'd been some talk of how the Hawaiian stores were selling out of boys' size 28 trunks, and some of the team theorized that maybe it heralded a turnaround—that kids were riding waves again, that surf was coming back. They were, and it was, but not in a way anybody was expecting. As McKnight sat on the sand at the Pipeline Masters surf contest that year with one of his designers, he saw a couple of *girls* walking along the beach. The girls were wearing string-bikini tops and boys' boardshorts slung low around the hips, and it looked so cool, so completely don't-give-a-shit new and individual and *right*, that . . . well, *boom*.

Yet how could Lisa ever be part of this sudden shift in Industry fortune, this approaching third boom? By now she was curled up on

Matt and me.

a couch at the ASP judges' rented mansion down the road from Pipeline, waiting for her events to get some swell, and sleeping. She was like a cat, indoors, dozing all day. This puzzled the ASP tour manager, Al Hunt, but only Lisa and Renato Hickel knew why. She was . . . pregnant.

Oh yes, she and Renato were an item. On the road in '92, Quiksilver's backing secured, feeling freer than ever, she'd gone to Jeffreys Bay for the first time in her life: Jeffreys Bay in South Africa, a stylist's ultimate wave, one of the spots Dave and the Georges had always talked about in those reverent tones, and it was all she'd imagined. Like Bells Beach and the beachbreaks of France, J-Bay was a wave made for her—those long lines, those fingertip bottom turns, that speed. Late one afternoon she paddled out and sat down the line from the main takeoff zone, while farther up, Renato, the ASP's head judge, patiently waited for his turn at a set wave. It came to him at last; everyone slid aside as happens when a surfer's waited long enough, Renato dropped down the face and began to run the wall down, and Lisa took straight off on him.

Flailing in the foam, climbing back on his board, Renato had to watch as she threw spray with every top turn and finally finished hundreds of yards away, turned . . . and waved.

"You're fucked!" the boys teased her that night, "Rule Number One—don't drop in on the head judge!"

A week later in Durban, Lisa lost her first heat and stared daggers at Renato as she trudged up the sands. That night he found her in a bar and said, "Do you know what's the fine for dropping in on a head judge?"

"No," said Lisa, wondering.

"You've got to go out to dinner with me," Renato told her.

Since she'd left Dave alone in San Luis Obispo, Lisa hadn't taken men too seriously. Her encounters with tour boys were funny, good-humored rather than predatory, though she does recall walking into a party at Lacanau in southwest France in August 1991, seeing young Australian rookie Matt Hoy, and more or less grabbing him by the scruff of the neck and marching him off.

Renato was something else. Renato Rodriguez Hickel, thirty years old, a charming, serious man from a big sprawling Brazilian Catholic family whose father was a well-known chemical engineer and university professor, had defied his own background to become a committed surfer, though not quite as dramatically as had Lisa. No one else in his family surfed, and when he started at thirteen, he found himself on the margins. Renato's competitive career stopped at the age of twenty when he discovered his girlfriend Monica was pregnant.

He knuckled down, took a job in a bank, and moved on to the Brazilian government's office of planning, feeding his surf stoke by helping to organize and judge regional events. In 1985, as Lisa made her fearful plans in Ormond Beach, Renato was offered a partnership in Brazil's major surf event promotor, Master Promotions. It was a career risk, but by now his family was resigned to their prodigal surfer, and his father gave Renato his backing both moral and financial.

This led swiftly to international events in Brazil, a part-time place on the ASP's judging panel, and in 1990, the sometimes unenviable job of ASP head judge.

Now Renato, serious and responsible and organized, was on the road with all the runaways, and it jarred his sensibilities. All the traveling began to split his relationship with Monica down its fault lines. At the same time, there was Lisa, whom he kept running into. He gave her advice about heat scores; he watched her in and out of the water.

"To me she was a bit of a loner," Renato says. "She was mysterious in that way. There was an attraction, she knew it and I knew it. It would kind of linger for a few months, then we would see each other again and it'd still be there."

To Lisa, Renato was all sorts of things. After he'd left South Africa that year, 1992, she wrote in her diary: "I can't say much, only that he has changed my life dramatically. I miss him extremely. It might not be easy for him to communicate with his wife now. I really am concerned about my feelings getting worked on this one. If he goes back to his wife, I will understand."

Later that year, in Europe, came these lines: "I am so in love that time stands still when I am with him. Every breath I take is slow and I breathe him deeper in to my soul."

On tour, tremendous suspicion greeted the relationship. Top girl pro and head judge? Even in loosey-goosey pro-surfing land, in the runaways' traveling circus, it was enough to trigger protests. Pam Burridge's partner, Mark Rabbidge, was most vocal in drawing attention to this latest apparent advantage of Pam's lethal young rival. Renato stopped judging Lisa's heats; a month or so later, to further alleviate the pressure, he stopped judging women's heats

Newport. Australia..

Variations on
my top turn.

I was 8 months pregnant in this photo.

altogether. He stopped even watching Lisa's heats, a restriction he found both stressful and a relief. Renato eventually took on Lisa's life in so many areas: lover, husband, mentor, manager, contract negotiator, newspaper-clipping keeper . . . later he would wonder if it was one of the reasons things didn't work between them.

In Hawaii, Lisa wasn't feeling too well and had a nagging thought as to why, so she went to the Foodland supermarket near Waimea Bay to get a pregnancy test kit, hoping nobody would be there and notice . . . though sure enough the checkout lady had to pick up the microphone and ask for "a price check on ClearBlue Easy" . . . so everyone could hear. Thanks a *lot*, checkout lady.

She found out and was instantly scared. This was Lisa's immediate reaction to pregnancy, each time it happened: fear of all the what-ifs. What if it wasn't mutual? What if something went wrong? Lisa never liked doctors, or hospitals. She and Renato decided not to tell anyone, but both did—Renato his fellow judges, Lisa her mother and a few tour buddies, including Wendy Botha. Wendy was used to Lisa coming up with surprises now and then, but this one was a doozy. Here she was, twenty-three years old, ranked fourth in the world, the surfer every girl thought was on some kind of collision course with a world championship, and pregnant? If it's right for you, she told her friend. She didn't really get it, but she didn't give up the secret,

even when Lisa surfed solid Sunset Beach in the contest the next day.

Lisa and Renato hatched a kind of plan: keep it quiet, surf as far as possible into the new year, try to preserve her ranking, play it by ear from there. This was easier than it might have been, because Lisa didn't swell with the pregnancy. She doesn't know if it was because she kept surfing, but the fetus sat high up under her rib cage, and people thought she'd just gained a little weight, what with all the nice food they assumed she must have been eating with Renato in Brazil. Her last heat was a quarterfinal at Bells Beach in late March. By then she was five and a half months pregnant; Renato later joked that Erica had surfed in a major pro event before she'd even learned to stand up.

Lisa was scared stiff of the idea of labor. She was glued to the Birth Channel, she knew every term in the lexicon, yet she didn't know

RIGHT: Erica as a baby.

anything at all. What, for instance, did "sharp pain" mean? When it came to the birth itself, all her fear of the whole thing evaporated, mainly because she was practically asleep. The doctors had given her an epidural—a spinal infusion of anesthetic drugs—to kill some of the pain, and it worked so well she can hardly recall what happened. She was even a little disappointed afterward, not to have been fully present when out came this little person, like a little monkey, with black fuzz all over, captured on video for posterity, and her saying groggily, "Oh my God! What's that? Where'd that come from?"

Thus emerged Miss Erica Andersen Hickel into the world at 1:54 A.M. on August 1, 1993, to Mr. and Mrs. Hickel. By then Renato and Lisa were official. They were married on March 18, a date Renato remembers better than Lisa. Actually, on that date thirteen years later, in 2006, Renato sends her a rude, funny e-mail. It shows a chimp with an Afro, and when you click on it the chimp says, "Hey baby, do you remember our anniversary and that time we had hot sex on the beach, and we have a beautiful daughter to remind you of that . . ."

So Brazilian, Renato. Lisa exerts her wicked wit in return, sends him an e-mail back with the same attachment, but with new words: "Sorry darling, it must not have been all that hot on the beach that time, I can't remember it. And *thank God* the daughter looks like me."

3. WINNING

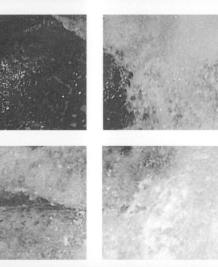

𝒜 HALF HOUR BEFORE SHE WINS HER FIRST WORLD PROFESSIONAL SURFING CHAMPIONSHIP, LISA IS ON THE BEACH AT NORTH NARRABEEN, AUSTRALIA, LATE 1994, ON A CLOUDY, WARM, HUMID MIDSUMMER SORT OF DAY, AND SHE IS TRYING TO STRETCH.

Rob Rowland Smith, her trainer, is holding her legs, and Andrew Murphy, Quiksilver's team manager, is leaning on her back, pushing her farther into the stretch. Lisa is nearly squealing with the pain of her injured lower back. "Forget the pain," Murphy mutters, "just forget it!" And she does, because every moment of pain up here on the beach means one less moment of pain out there, in the water, where it counts.

One heat stands between Lisa and the world title, one heat against a girl named Yvonne Rogencamp, who just happens to be the hottest woman surfer in North Narrabeen's long rich surf history. One heat, Yvonne, and a back injury that, despite all the attention and training in the known surfing universe, won't get better. It wasn't even such a big deal at first—just a tweak low in the spine during a surf at Huntington—but Lisa, busy being Mom and winning heats, didn't take full care of it, and the pain slowly worsened, and Pauline Menczer, naughty Pauline the dogged title defender, began to chase her down, whittling away Lisa's massive points lead. As the second-to-last event of the year approached, the Diet Coke Classic,

PAGES 92–93: This was my first big win. I had $140 to my name and won $8,000. I went back to California and bought a stereo and a waterbed.

FEAR-
LESS-
NESS

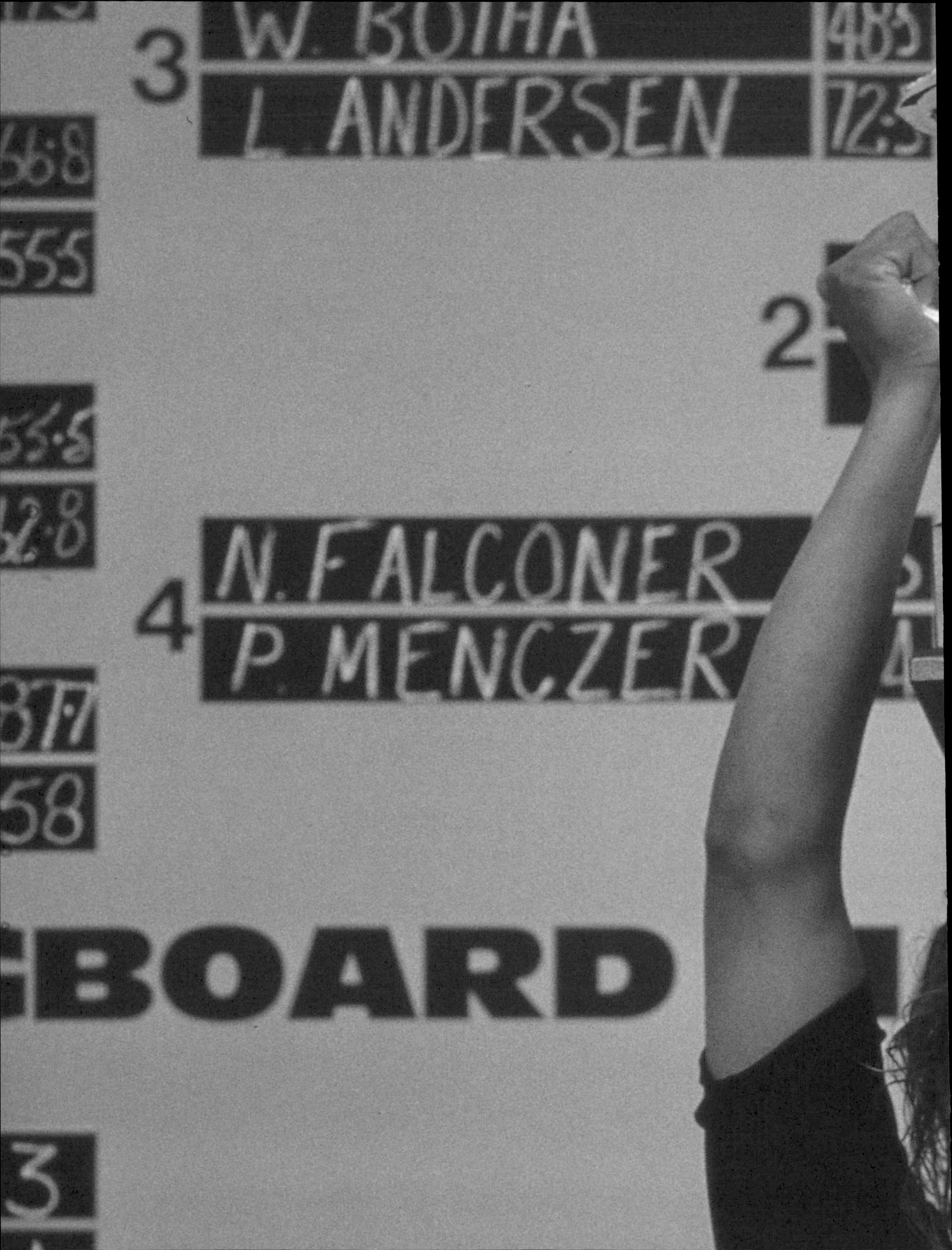
3
W. BOTHA
L. ANDERSEN
72.5
2
4
N. FALCONER
P. MENCZER
BOARD

Pauline was within range, and Lisa hadn't surfed for over a month. Instead she'd been engaged in all the machinery of pro-athlete rehabilitation: deep-water running, swimming, Janice Raymond taking her to sports physiotherapist Malcolm Brown's office at 5:30 A.M., a three-hour there and back drive every morning for a month, heat, cold, electrotherapy, Janice and Lisa chanting at each other, "We're doing this 'cause we're gonna win! . . ."

At last, two days before the contest, she has a two-wave surf at a beach near the event site. Nothing bad happens. The next day, another surf, about a half hour this time. Then, down to North Narrabeen. "You've got to shut out all the noise," Murph and Rob had drummed into her. "Shut out what's happening around you. Focus on the job." She paddles out, gets the edge on wave scores, but Yvonne fights back and takes a slight lead. With a minute to go, Lisa needs a minor score, a 4-point-something out of 10. Now Lisa is paddling against the rip in the Narrabeen Alley, that famously destructive rip, furious, frustrated, because no matter how strongly she paddles, the rip is dragging her out to sea at exactly the same pace, so despite all the effort, she stays in one spot. Forty seconds left. A bump crosses the rip and picks her up. She's on it. It develops and reaches clear water past the rip as an actual wave. Lisa stands up, turns, cuts back, turns again, works the wave, rides it all the way to the beach. Up in the surf club, Renato and Erica are playing together, Renato doing his best to ignore what's happening out there in the

rip, but then Pam Burridge leans in the window and yells at him: "She's got it!"

The score is 6-something. The little wave has lifted her to the crown.

GREAT SURFERS ALL LEARN HOW TO WIN IN DIFFERENT WAYS, and yet

the result in the end is always oddly similar: they start winning, and keep winning, and they don't stop until whatever it is that caused them to start has run its course through their hearts and bodies and minds.

Lisa learned to win the only way she'd ever learn anything: her way.

She'd been coached. Had she ever been coached. After Comen and his heat drills and video sessions, there'd been Parmenter and their video sessions, Parmenter's confidence in her skills, his surfboard designing and knowledge and advice. Then for a while there'd been Derek Hynd, the ex–pro surfer and fan of Lisa's who'd been hired by Rip Curl to coach their pro team. Derek showed her some clever things, like riding a longer board in the morning warm-up sessions before events so she'd catch more waves, but his ruthless solitary coaching methods drove her crazy. He'd sit there on the beach and silently make reams of notes, then when she came in after a heat he'd say: "What did you do wrong? Do you know? Write it down." If she made a really big mistake, he'd leave her a note and not speak to her till the next event. Once at Bells she lost a heat and came in to find Hynd had left the beach; in front of her towel, one word was written in the sand in big letters: LOSER.

Then came Renato, of course, the head judge, with his minutely accurate understanding of rides and scores—Renato, who, of all the men who tried to coach her, knew just how easily Lisa could win pretty much any heat she entered . . . if only she *would.* "I cannot believe you gave that wave away!" he would tell her as they drove off from another slipup, until Lisa would want to jump out of the moving car in rage and frustration. Because she knew already.

Lacanau Beach Pro, pre-Erica.

Every time she made an error in a heat, she knew immediately what she'd done and the consequences of it.

Lisa's classic error was a simple one, yet at the same time it was strange and puzzling, both to her and to the onlooker. It would often occur well into a heat, when she needed a serious score of some kind. Waves would be coming, rearing into the takeoff zone, and she would select one and begin to paddle, then for some reason, just before she'd pick up the wave, she would stop and let it go. Her body would just . . . stop. Her mind would be telling her, *Oh no, you're paddling too early,* or it would say, *Uh-oh, you're paddling too slowly for it, you're going over the falls.* It would be time for an instant of decision, that moment at the start of a ride so familiar to all lifelong surfers, and in that instant, just for an instant, her mind would reject it, and her body would betray her, and the wave would slip past. In that instant she was afraid: *What if I don't get the score, what if I can't?* The instant of fear, half-suppressed, half-emerged, would leave her sitting out there. *Let's just think about it some more.*

What coach could help her with that? In any case, she could never really commit to a coach. Partly it was just that she hated to be criticized; perhaps her stubborn instincts were telling her she had to figure it out by herself. Partly it was something else, something she didn't know back then but sees clearly enough now: "I think every single coach I had reminded me of my dad, so I just didn't want to listen to

them. It was another chance to rebel against someone."

The contests were always so social, something Lisa loved—after all, she was part of the brethren, and it mattered to her that she was liked.

But then she started doing things herself. She started watching heats. She'd try to find a place around the beach, a little hiding place, put a sweatshirt hood over her head and her sunglasses on so nobody would know who she was, not talking to anyone, and she'd sit for eight hours and watch heat after heat, feeling kind of like a bitch for not being more social . . . but it

worked. After a day like that, she'd understand the surf spot, she'd have a feel for the rhythm of heats and the way the contest was evolving. She worked on her routines, making sure everything right before and right after a heat happened exactly the same way, even to the extent that she'd rewax her boards a week before each contest, so she could get her feet set in the wax without it being too fresh, or too slippery from overuse. She began to find it was possible to get into a place where she could turn everything off, shut out every possible distraction. In one of her favorite films, the baseball movie *For Love of the Game,* the hero, a pitcher named Billy Chapel,

ABOVE: Covered up in Japan.
RIGHT: Sunset Beach.

does just that, shuts out the thousands of people yelling at him from the bleachers and goes into an inner world where nothing exists but the simple details of batter, diamond, pitch.

Ian Cairns, Lisa's old NSSA mentor, had another theory about her. Surfing, theorizes Ian, attracts messed-up people because of its simplicity. It's easy! Throw on a pair of shorts, paddle out, surf, smoke some dope, be with friends. The freedom is largely a freedom from the pressure to have a real act.

Cairns thought successful competitive surfers got beyond this by applying themselves, learning the thousand tricks of the trade through hard work and personal discipline. Lisa, he thought, was a surfer of the rarest type—the instinctive genius, the type who performs best when things are entirely simplified. She was destined to perform only when she could see the events as being simple things, where all she had to do was paddle out and catch waves.

Cairns is half right in his assessment, yet he's only half right. For Lisa is a surfer of an even rarer type—an instinctive genius who is also a woman. For her to see the events as simple things, something else had to come along that would overwhelm them utterly with its importance, that would make paddling out and catching waves seem like utter freedom, contest or no contest.

MOTHER-HOOD

LISA, OCTOBER 2005:

Erica Andersen Hickel is darting through the house in Huntington Beach, humming, hopping up and down, singing something to herself. She has a friend over from her new school—another new school in a list of schools Erica has attended in her twelve gypsy years. Her friend's name is Taylah, a nice enough girl who is kind of trailing around behind Erica, in her thrall, which is no surprise, for Erica is definitely the center of attention. "You guys want a drink?" asks Lisa, vaguely soccer-momish all of a sudden, and her daughter waves dismissedly. "Maybe," she says. "Taylah! C'mere!" And the girls are gone upstairs, chasing one of the family cats.

In a few months, when she writes her reply to Renato's anniversary chimp-mail, Lisa won't be entirely accurate in her assessment of Erica's looks. Erica does have her mother's bones—the clean line of the jaw, the Danish cheekbones—but she also has her father's hazel-green eyes

Erica and me in Hawaii.

and wide-open features. Something about her appearance screams the Stage, and indeed she's already being drafted for auditions by teen-talent production companies. Buried somewhere in the many hours of videotape shot of this little family's life is a short clip of Erica at five, wandering with her mom around their Ormond Beach home. The cameraman asks Erica what she'd like to do when she grows up, and she says brightly, "I wanna be a model, just like Mommy!" Sardonic chuckle from Mom.

For Lisa, Erica's birth was like a line drawn in the sand, an initiation. Bruce Raymond says he always had a sense of where childbirth might take this half-formed champion. By this time, 1993, she'd forced her way to fourth in the world, yet the few heat wins from there to the world championship can seem like a gap impossible to bridge. "She had so much natural ability, but she didn't know how to turn the switch on," he recalls. "You could feel that thing about a really talented sports person, their myopia, how they draw on everyone around them. Lisa was trying to focus on where she was going, but she couldn't pull it all together. . . . I think people

thought her surfing career was over because she was pregnant. But to me, I thought, This is gonna work. She'll have the baby, she'll get that new maturity into her head, there's no working into it, it's not a three-year program, it's *boom!* Not only will she come good physically, but her brain would do the thing that needed to happen."

Lisa, with all her stubborn hopeful energy, had the sensationally optimistic idea that she'd go straight back to her life, to the traveling circus, and Erica would simply become part of that life. Three days after the birth, she and Erica were in Miami, arranging a passport. Twelve days afterward, they were in Lacanau, France, and Lisa was surfing in a heat at a major event. The plan had been to show up, enter, take the prize money and ratings points, but not to *surf*. No way. Two weeks after having a kid? The waves were large and heavy and confusing, the way a French beachbreak can be. Lisa was out of condition, her timing off, but she let the ocean slam and push her around anyway. She wanted to surf. She didn't get far, but she didn't come last either. A week later she surfed in another event, at Hossegor, 150 miles south of Lacanau, where the surf was even bigger. She duck-dove and duck-dove until she was exhausted, again didn't get far . . . again, didn't come last.

The baggage was crazy. Every time she'd see a store carrying something she'd thought might make traveling with baby a little easier, Lisa had charged in and bought it, with the result that she and Renato went from

RIGHT: Erica on my hip after I won the 1994 Lacanau Pro in France.

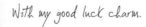
With my good luck charm.

packing a duffel bag and boardbag each to a *lot* of bags, a stroller, a folding travel cot, plus all the detritus and overwhelming detail of early parenthood, the bottles and diapers and formula and wipes. Plus the endless need to plan every minute in the existence of this small creature, who'd suddenly appeared in your life and who now mattered more than anything you might care to be doing at any particular time. Lisa would bring Erica down to the judging tower at the contests, recruiting a couple of the guys to help carry the stroller across the sand, then once Erica was settled up there next to Renato, sure enough, the horn would blow to end or start a heat, and Erica would be wide awake and yelping. After a while, she grew used to the heat hooter and slept right through.

People oohed and aahed over Erica, and later, as she grew up and began running around the contests like she owned them, Erica would have a substantial number of tour pros, wives, girlfriends, and even Lisa's opposition tangled around her little finger. But in that first year or so of traveling, worrying about formula mixes, and hoping Renato would get up for the two A.M. feeding, motherhood brought it home to Lisa again and again: the ease, the luxury even, of being able to attend to surfing and contests and all the stuff she'd once thought so difficult. She'd get an hour to surf, and wouldn't want to come in. She'd say, "No! Another five

seventh when two other pros—Jodie Cooper and Lisa's old friend Wendy Botha—retired. In 1994 she made five of the first six event finals, winning two, including the big new U.S. Open at Huntington Beach, where she'd once watched the surf stars so eagerly through the plastic contest-site fencing. Six months after that she was the champ.

After that day at Narrabeen, that winning day, Lisa did something Janice Raymond couldn't believe: she decided to buy a suit. C'mon, she told Janice, we're going shopping, and they went to Sydney's Oxford Street, a long untidy street filled with very bohemian yet not so quietly expensive stores—couture to the eyeballs! Nothing like Ormond Beach—and Lisa picked out a beautiful elegant Armani pinstripe, the kind you see on famous actresses when they're visiting the U.N. to be made honorary ambassadors for something. Three thousand dollars, and Lisa just put a credit card down on the counter like it was nothing. Lisa saying, in a way: I'm a winner now, I'm on the red carpet, this is who I am, where I belong. *Well,* thought Janice, *I guess she figures she's earned it.*

She'd already been back to Florida, more than once. The first time, tentatively, around

minutes." Instead of a torment, surfing heats became an escape.

"It shed the light on what I was missing," she says today. "Every moment in the water was precious to me."

Two months after Erica was born, Lisa went to Japan with a new quiver of boards, from the California-based Brazilian designer Xanadu, and made a final. She finished the year of Erica's birth ranked ninth in the world, hurdling to

Thanksgiving 1986, to surf the U.S. Trials for the World Contest team. The contest was at Melbourne Beach, an hour or so south of Ormond, and her mother and little brother, Lorraine and Scotty, decided they'd meet her down there for a Thanksgiving dinner. Though they were now divorced, Lorraine invited Lisa's father, John, and he came down too. Lisa had a pet with her, a white rat she'd named Hey You; she'd kept Hey You in her pocket on the plane all the way from California.

Then she was there during her pregnancy with Erica, which Lisa, truth to tell, quite enjoyed. She went home to Ormond Beach, to her mother, and all the pressure of competition and tour life dropped away. She sunbathed, swam, watched TV, ate, relaxed. She and Renato even visited with John Andersen, whom Renato liked a lot, seeing now for himself where Lisa got her sharp humor and her Danish cheekbones. That was something else about being pregnant for Lisa: at least partly, it reconnected her with her parents, especially with Lorraine. If falling pregnant when she did seemed odd at the time, or seems odd even now, consider another coincidence, natural, generational: Lorraine had her first child, Eddie, at almost the same age, twenty-three.

Now, though, Lisa had actually done what she'd written on the note she'd left on the pillow of the house in Bosarvey Avenue: become someone who, at the time, she hadn't even known existed. Imagine the confidence! Imagine, in that circumstance, being able to say to everyone: "See? I did it! I did what I said!" Emboldened, Lisa went back to Ormond Beach and took out a mortgage on a house near her mother's apartment. Lorraine was increasingly involved in her daughter's and granddaughter's lives, babysitting and even occasionally traveling to events, and Lisa increasingly allowed herself to imagine something new: If she could be married, if she could have a child, win a world title, wear an Armani suit, then surely now she could put some sort of stake into a future, wave a finger at the past.

At home in Florida recouping from back injury.

BOOM TIME

What was Roxy worth now, in the summers of 1995 and '96, as this small storm of girl-power surf history blew gales through the beaches and malls of the United States? What had happened while Lisa was learning to win?

Roxy boardshort hangtag.

Surf girls had been ignored for almost the entire existence of organized surfing; nothing prepared the surfing establishment for the girls of the Roxy generation. They were nothing like anyone in modern surfing—in modern anything—had seen. They were the innocuous result of a freed-up feminized wealthy Western world, girls who were uncritically into doing what they wanted, and not overly concerned with self-doubt in the process. Girls who, thanks to Title IX legislation, had grown up playing soccer and T-ball next to boys, or just in rabid, muddy packs of their own devising. Girls whose surfing fathers wanted the best for them. As these girls surged into surfing, into the *idea* of surfing, into lineups from Rocky Point, Hawaii, to Santa Cruz, California, the largely male-run surf industry largely

The Ponce Inlet groms. Florida. 1995.

panicked. Nobody understood this market, nobody knew what to call the clothes they were suddenly having to make; most of the companies just stuck "Girl" on the end of their brand names and hoped for the best. Bob Hurley, for instance, who ran Billabong in the United States and eventually left to begin his own eponymous label, wouldn't even go there; Hurley stayed out of the girls' market for years. The surf media bewilderedly ran pictures of and interviews with some of these amazing sleek new-era girls, Daize Shayne and Sanoe Lake (nicknamed "the Rocky Pointer Sisters" in *Surfing* magazine), and the long-limbed NSSA junior Veronica Kay, while girls-only surf mags began popping up, run by older women surfers with a certain "told ya so!" glitter in their tone.

In the center of this, in the eye of the storm, having somehow survived the early 1990s surf-industry purge as a patch on short denim skirts, sat Roxy. It now fell into league with its natural market, the only distinct girls' surf-action label on earth. Bob McKnight put former Raisins swimwear boss Randy Hild in charge.

Randy Hild. Godfather.

At first, along with its cropped tees and athletic-yet-cute swimwear, Roxy produced a basic surf short, the likes of which McKnight had seen slung around the hips of those girls on the beach at Pipeline. But Lisa had the idea that a woman could do better than men's-style shorts. Her newfound confidence urged her to push Roxy's designers toward trunks cut to female lines, shorter, curved to fit hip and upper thigh, to free up movement in the water and on a board.

Thus appeared the Roxy boardshort, first authentic original garment of the era . . . and while Randy Hild unleashed the New York fashion photographer Dewey Nicks on beach houses full of these young, not-quite-grown girls, these avatars of the Roxy generation, there was always Lisa in the background—always Lisa's slashing turns, always Hornbaker's extraordinary, vivid photography of his favorite subject. Lisa could look into Jeff's lens in a way no one else could quite persuade her to do.

Lisa gave it all a core. Behind the still-forming Roxy image stood this figure whose power and skill you couldn't doubt.

Infamous poster for Roxy boardsports. 1994.

By 1997 the label was selling around $40 million, a tenfold increase in just over two years. Today, McKnight says, turnover is ten times that again and more. Indeed, it could be said, girls' surfwear and activewear saved an industry that never saw it coming. Some storm.

In 1994, the ASP women's world tour consisted of eleven events and $295,000 in prize money, triple the cash of 1987, Lisa's first year. By 1997, the numbers had exploded out to over $530,000. Wendy Botha was gone now, Lisa's blonde power-surfing predecessor, the girl who might have been Lisa if the rest of the world had been running a few years ahead of schedule. After being surprised by Lisa's pregnancy, incidentally, Wendy had done something that surprised Lisa at least as much: she'd posed nude in the Australian version of *Playboy* magazine—a move no Roxy-generation girl would've considered for a second. Not long afterward, injured and sick of the travel, Wendy had retired and married her pro-footballer boyfriend, Brent. In Wendy's place came driven young Australian Layne Beachley, the girl who craved Lisa's

crown; Layne, who, for all her dominant competitive skills, couldn't ever quite match the Andersen fingertip touch on a wave.

Lisa's surfing grew in response. She would win repeatedly at the same places: Bells Beach

CLOCKWISE FROM TOP LEFT: At the 1995 ASP awards banquet.
Walking up the hill after a heat at Bells.
Reunion Island. 1995. A scary place but I always did well there for some reason.
Gold Coast. 1992.
Bells. 1992. I had just signed with Quiksilver and this was my first win in front of the Quiksilver friends.
Portugal. 1997. I had already won my fourth world title by this point.

in Australia, Lacanau in France, St. Leu on Réunion Island, places with which she felt an emotional as much as a technical surfing connection. She began to stretch the limits and lines of her style, letting the tail drift out of top turns, riding toward the standards of the world tour's new-era boys, Ross Williams and Shane Dorian and Pat O'Connell and their staggeringly talented leader, that other Floridian, Kelly Slater. When stuck-in-the-mud surf-mag journalists asked her if she wanted to surf like a man, she laughed and told them what had become obvious to her: "It doesn't have to be feminine or masculine."

In Hawaii in 1995, she got into these tube duels with Rochelle Ballard. Never a great tuberider, Lisa disliked the classic North Shore surf-photography stretch from Backdoor Pipeline to Off-the-Wall—the exposed rock reef had her thinking too much about consequences. Rochelle, a born charger, teased and encouraged her into sessions, and Lisa began drawing lines into places on waves she'd always avoided. The photographers went crazy.

Grajagan in Indonesia showed her where her limits lay; G-land and later Teahupo'o, in Tahiti, where she once left an event site on a stretcher, swearing never to surf there again. These heavy hollow waves in unfamiliar waters, with their supernatural curving menace, were beyond her ability to sense a line through a

ABOVE: The gang at Rochelle's place in Hawaii. 1995.

wave. "Why is it that C. J. and Damien [Hobgood] can just paddle out at Teahupo'o and . . . catch waves, set waves, and charge?" she wonders today. "What is that?"

Sunset Beach, too, threw her. She still regrets never winning an event in Hawaii; in this way also she is like Tom Curren, who only ever won one, and never during a world-title run. Sunset got her with its huge, wide-open spaces—all that watery room between waves! How would you ever know where to go? Lisa would paddle out and sit there, wishing for a wave. "I knew one would come to me! I'd sit and think, okay, 7.5 or whatever, it *will* come to me this time! And it never would." Sunset is both a

commitment and a tease; you've got to take your 150 wipeouts to understand it, and Lisa's stubbornness didn't let her take its bait.

The prize money was up, but the endorsement money was another matter. Lisa's original contract with Quiksilver, through Bruce Raymond, had been $500 a month, and she'd grabbed it with both hands. The figure had climbed since then, but now she was world champion. She employed a manager, Mike Kingsbury of MKM in Huntington Beach, and sent him in pursuit of more. When Bruce suggested to Kingsbury that her Roxy salary rise from $50,000 to $70,000, she was less than impressed. "Maybe they could give the extra to the owners and have them

This sequence is from a Rochelle-inspired session at Backdoor, 1996.

subscribe to all the magazines around the world," she wrote to Kingsbury sarcastically. She was even less impressed when she accidentally got a glimpse of Rochelle Ballard's salary check from another company and realized she wasn't even the best-paid woman pro.

Bruce Raymond chalked it up to the times—surf companies were still wrestling with the very idea of a top girl pro being worth anything, much less a six-figure salary. Things improved in the ensuing years, but for Lisa, it still rankles. She was leading the Roxy generation toward better things, but would she ever reap the benefits? She didn't know.

Between events, and brief stays in Ormond Beach and Sydney, she and Renato lived in Florianópolis, Brazil. After only eighteen months, the marriage was already beginning to fray at the edges. Lisa loved Renato's parents and extended family, and she tried to fit in, learning Portuguese well enough to understand it, if not to speak it perfectly. She thought Florianópolis beautiful, with nice waves, and sometimes she could surf with the local superstar pro, Flavio Padaratz. But Brazil frightened her, with its third-world feel, the little kids begging for money in the street, the feeling that anything might happen. She stayed indoors a lot and watched television, and called friends on the phone. And when Renato was there, his natural habits of neatness preyed on her nerves. She felt he wanted her to be someone else, someone who'd put makeup on and go out on his arm and look pretty. To her horror, Renato was beginning to remind her of her father. "Maybe it's normal in a marriage but it's too much for me," she wrote in her diary after a disagreement. "I am fragile. I get afraid. I want Erica to grow up with parents. The original family. There is a part of me that will always believe in keeping together—forever. Give me strength."

Increasingly, for companionship, she turned to the people she knew best, and who knew her in ways others might never quite manage: her fellow runaways.

Steve Sherman took this picture while I was waiting in a car park in Biarritz. France. 1994.

Renato and Erica. 1994.

Erica and I used to have "who could make the ugliest face" contests. I always won.

Erica in Hawaii. 1995.

Erica and me. Hawaii.

CLOCKWISE FROM TOP: *Tahiti boat trip, in good company. Kelly and me at ASP banquet, 1996. girls in the Gold Coast between sessions. V.K. and me in Kauai, Hawaii.*

RUNAWAYS

DURANBAH, AUSTRALIA, MARCH 2006:

Megan Abubo is sitting in the shade of a casuarina tree on a crazily hot day, three hours past winning her third-round heat at the Roxy Pro, and stealing little glances out at the ocean. Little wind-fanned waves are crumbling up and down a flat stretch of sand that today, oddly, looks a little like Ormond Beach.

Dark-haired, dark-eyed Hawaiian Megan, powerful and cool the way surfers from the sport's homeland tend to be, is a wonderful type—the girl Lisa liberated, a younger rider of the Roxy wave.

Megan was in tenth grade, surfing Waikiki as a matter of course as Waikiki kids do, when she first saw Lisa, on a five-minute MTV sports clip. She suddenly thought, *Girls can make money from this! You could be a pro surfer! I could be!* She watched the clip every day until she was eighteen years old. By then she'd long since met Lisa, on the beach at Huntington

CLOCKWISE FROM TOP: Occy. G-land. early '90s.
My heroes. G-land. Java.
Fiji surf trip.

during the U.S. Open contest. What does Megan remember? "She was pretty scary, actually. She was very competitive. I was just a kid and it was overwhelming because she was my idol. I think she was scared of me because I was such an amped grom—you know when you meet those groms who just love you? And that's what I was when I came up against her. She was nice, she was really just . . . serious."

Back then, by way of contrast, Lisa remembers a cocky, psyched-up grommet giving her the tough-girl preheat stare down, Hawaiian-style, and at the time, she started laughing inside. *You're trying to flip me out, but you're flipping yourself out instead,* Lisa, a bit surprised then to realize she wasn't the new-comer anymore, that she was suddenly kind of . . . grown-up.

Megan was the only girl on the Hawai-ian Quiksilver team—another girl among boys. When those first Roxy boardshorts hit the warehouse, in 1993, she leaped into them. Kids at school wanted to *mug* her for those board-shorts. "I'm a pretty feminine girl, you know, I never wanted to be a macho-ey girl. I was always raised with what Rell [Sunn] would tell me, like be graceful, be a girl, and Lisa could do that. She could be so feminine on a wave yet so radical, and it really changed the face of our sport that she could do that. I can still be the girl that I am and yet still rip, and she helped me see that.

"And still to this day when I watch Lisa surf . . . I went on a surf trip with her this last summer and she did two of the best turns of the entire trip and surfed better than anybody else in the lineup . . . she's amazing. She's ten years older than me, it's amazing that she can surf as good as she did back then. Yet she's got a really good attitude to surfing and she knows she's really talented, and she just goes with it, she expresses herself really well in the water."

Up walks Rochelle Ballard, through the casuarinas, squinting through the heat: Rochelle, thirty-five, from Kauai via Sunset Beach, Oahu, five foot four, skeptical, funny, and like all the best girl surfers these days, confident as hell. "God, man, it's freakin' hot!" she says, looking at Megan. "Was it your idea to sit here?"

Rochelle and Lisa first met way back in 1986, when they briefly trained under Glenn

Big turns in Indo. 2005.

O. Kirkby. They surfed a heat at Oceanside, California, while Kirkby filmed. Later, around 1991, when Rochelle began to surf as a pro, she thought Lisa had a cold unapproachability about her, especially toward the other women pros. But after a time, she saw "a real feisty, mysterious sort of girl. It's funny, 'cause you look at her and if she doesn't have a smile on her face, she'll have this little sorta smirk. And you look and go, *hmmmm,* you're not sure about her. Then she'll give you this smile and it's so radiant, and that laugh that's so, like, it just gets you right here in your heart.

"She has just such good energy about her. She's really a warm person. She's had some adversity in her life, at times created it but at other times a victim of circumstance, but no matter what she's gone through, she's always stayed that soft person inside and warmhearted."

The pair ponder Lisa's taste in men. She likes an older man, from what Rochelle has noticed, though she'll still talk about boys. Megan agrees: distinguished gentlemen. "She probably lets us know a little bit more than them. Being her good friends, we see her soft spots. Things that make her tick."

"She'll probably close herself off from men a little more."

"Or does a bit of the flirtatious cat-and-mouse thing with 'em—"

"Yeah! Exactly! That's what it is." Rochelle is grinning. "She just plays with 'em."

"She doesn't do that with us. So we probably know a bit more."

Ever seriously been worried about her for any reason? "Oh no," says Rochelle, her grin turning to laughter. "She's always been one for survival and making the most of her life. She's always got great people looking out for her. . . . I don't think it's a question of worrying about her, it's more been to see her complete all of her goals and be happy in her life, and enjoy all the things she's created for herself."

Rochelle figures it was age and time that opened Lisa, that and winning. "And really having the right people come along in her life. She felt comfortable and had similar tastes and enjoyed their company and that's what it's all about. Once she started hanging out with me and Meg and a few of the girls on tour, we just had a lot of fun together and that's what it really boils down to—people you can relate to."

Now a coincidence that isn't: like Lisa, both Rochy and Megan come from broken homes. Rochelle's parents divorced when she was young, she herself is divorced from her filmmaking former husband, Bill, and she now has three half siblings from her mom's second marriage. Megan's father left early, and her mother died when Megan was in her teens. "Lisa and I talk about it quite a bit," says Megan. "She helps me out at some rough times. We talk about it a lot. But we try to be and stay really positive, especially when you're out on trips and enjoying yourself. Like anything, it coulda been worse, so I think she and I sorta see things like that.

"That's what's good about her, she tries to move forward and so do I. We don't try to dwell on the past too much." Like all the runaways, like Rochelle, like Lisa herself, Megan is looking for the good.

Veronica and me on The Crossing. Best roommate ever.

ONE OF THE WORLD'S
GREATEST SURFERS LIKES TO DRESS
IN WOMEN'S CLOTHING.

Lisa Andersen, "Style X work", ©1996 Oakley, Inc.

FAMOUS

So now it is a decade and more after she fled the blind-drawn house in Ormond Beach, and Lisa, the Virginia farm girl turned runaway turned unlikely surf star turned mother turned world champion turned cult leader of a girl-power generation, is famous . . . famous in a way you can be only in America, with the *Good Morning America* and *Today* show appearances, the trade shows, the glossy magazine spreads, the honed mechanisms of fame.

She is famous and she is single again. In April 1995, all the irritations within the marriage boil over, and she makes one of her Decisions. Renato pleads, he tries to understand, he sleeps on the floor beside her bed. She is adamant. Though she's sure it's for the best, she almost cringes to recall her cruelty.

"We didn't argue much," says Renato. "I used to boast about that to my friends. Even when we separated, it was very practical, like, Okay, how do we handle this? Maybe we should have argued more. Our relationship was soooo new, and I just thought, Oh no, I've just had nine years of trying to make something else work, I don't want to argue again. So it was

**FEAR-
LESS-
NESS**

totally my doing." Ah, Renato, always taking responsibility.

On December 24, 1995, he writes Lisa a letter, a sad, apologetic, grateful letter, thanking her for Erica and the good things they shared, wishing her well. Lisa stays tough, though she writes a note, a song lyric, in her diary around the same time:

> This is our last goodbye
> I'd hate to feel that love between us die
> But it's over, just hear this and then I'll go
> You gave me more to live for, more than
>   you'll ever know

She is famous, yet her circle of friends remains tight. In 1995 her Christmas card list reads: Hornbaker, Tom Carroll, Oakley staff, Quiksilver Australia and USA, the Raymonds, Aunt Shane, Mom, Duane, Renato, Peter and Jan Wilson, Rochelle and Bill Ballard, Megan Abubo. This is her Australian year: working out in the mornings with Quiksilver's house athletic trainer Rob Rowland Smith, playing with Avalon boys Colin Bernasconi and Shane Allen in the afternoons, wallowing in the luxurious freedom that comes with being a visitor, without ties.

In 1996, her real Fame Year, she spends a total of 80 days at home in Ormond Beach and 285 on the road. Mike Kingsbury books her up and down the East Coast, and she collects a reported 360 million media "impressions"; theoretically now at least, she is more famous than that other child of Floridian waters, Kelly Slater. She makes the cover of *Surfer* magazine,

hailed with a line almost redundant by now: "Lisa Andersen surfs better than you." She is interviewed in *Surfing* magazine by journalist Jamie Brisick, a tour compadre from way back, who tells her she's "become a sex symbol." *Really?* replies Lisa. *You're not aware of it?* inquires Brisick. *No, not really,* she says, in her slightly wicked, slightly Southern drawl, *not at all. I'm not that type.*

Nobody in the surf media mocks the women anymore—nobody, that is, except Australia's *Tracks* magazine, in an article by the mag's tour correspondent Paul Sargeant entitled "Women in Surfing: Do They Belong in the Bedroom or the Barrel?" "They were built to love and caress and be feminine, just as the good Lord intended," writes Sargeant, who's

Japan trade show.

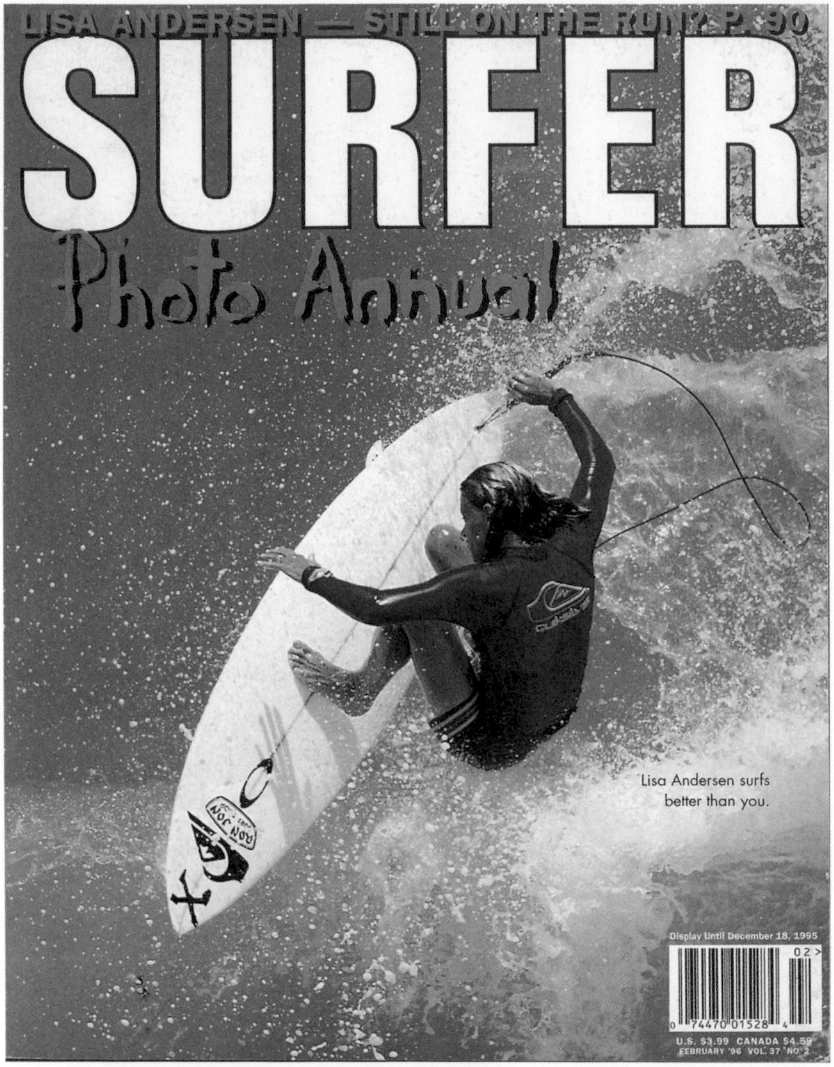

SURFER

Photo Annual

Lisa Andersen surfs better than you.

Display Until December 18, 1995

U.S. $3.99 CANADA $4.50
FEBRUARY '96 VOL. 37 NO. 2

0 74470 01528 4

02 >

SOUL

motion

spring ★★★★ e

+extra poster

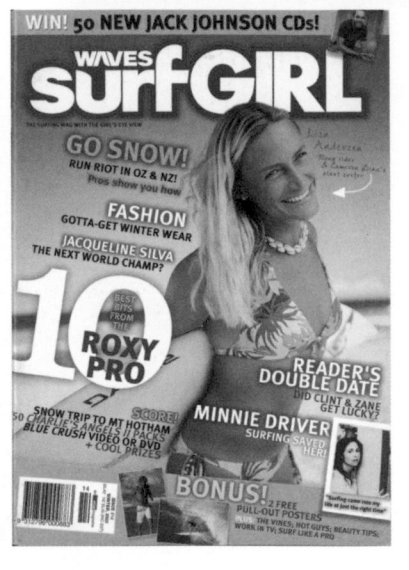

WIN! 50 NEW JACK JOHNSON CDs!

WAVES

surfGIRL

GO SNOW!
RUN RIOT IN OZ & NZ!
Pros show you how

FASHION
GOTTA-GET WINTER WEAR

JACQUELINE SILVA
THE NEXT WORLD CHAMP?

10
BEST SHOTS FROM THE
ROXY PRO

READER'S DOUBLE DATE
DID CLINT & ZANE GET LUCKY?

MINNIE DRIVER
SURFING SAVED HER!

SCORE!
SNOW TRIP TO MT HOTHAM
BLUE CRUSH VIDEO OR DVD
+ COOL PRIZES

BONUS! 2 FREE PULL-OUT POSTERS

Spring 1998 $4.95

ProSurfing

The Official ASP World Tour Guide

The Greatest Ever
KELLY SLATER & LISA ANDERSEN
World Champions

INSIDE:
Picture Profiles:
Top 44 Men & Top 11 Women
Perspective: Tom Carroll
Conversations with the Masters
Women's Tour Takes Center Stage
ASP's Cultural Revolution

JANUARY 1998

Condé Nast
Sports
FOR WOMEN

Go For the Goal!
How to *Really* Change Your Workout, Your Body and Your Life

The Top 10 Sporty Spas

Metabolism Makeover Plus: Do Vitamins Work?

Yoga!
The Joy of Flex...

The Happy Hooker and Other Fish Stories

World Champion Surfer
Lisa Andersen

The 1997
Sportswomen of the Year
Portfolio by Annie Leibovitz

Lisa Andersen's
Signature Shoe

reef

covered the world tour for fifteen years without ever paddling out for a surf. Later that year he declares his intention to start—whereupon Lisa and Rochelle hunt down the board he's decided to start on, and wax the entire thing: deck, rails, bottom, fins, the lot.

In the midst of the Fame Year, she is interviewed by Martha Sherrill for *Outside* magazine. The feature is later called "Gidget Kicks Ass." The intelligent Sherrill reports Lisa as "oddly impenetrable, closed down, as if the personality of a seventeen-year-old linebacker had been grafted onto her feminine psyche." She describes Lisa at the finish of a contest at Huntington: "Andersen says hello, shrugs, and walks on. Lorraine trudges behind her, pulling Erica. It's like a Day of the Dead procession all the way back to The Shores [motel], Andersen and her entourage of responsibility: her mom, Erica, the surfboard, the stroller, the toys, the drawing board and crayons, the bag of snacks."

Lisa is still her mother's daughter, her aunts' niece, Virginia farm girl. She loves the

success, but is she able to enjoy the fame? In Australia, for instance, Erica comes down with chicken pox. Kind of hard to take fame seriously when you're coming home to that stuff.

In 1997 she has one farcical heat, a throwback heat, in Japan, against a local rookie wild card. The surf is small beachbreak, and Lisa barely catches a wave. Rochelle and Megan and the rest of them are watching as the world champ drifts aimlessly through the lineup, hardly needing a score but not getting a thing. *What is she doing?* they wonder. The rookie wins and comes in practically speechless with excitement; Lisa comes in looking dark but laughing to herself, thinking, *Well, at least that girl's having a peak experience.* Megs and Rochy know better than to hassle her about it.

Other than that, she is unstoppable. No hesitation left, no confusion, nothing but a perfect surfing talent taken to its natural logical level. She surfs now in beautifully timed curves, having arrived at the place all great surfers reach—a place of utter assurance, the style tweaks incorporated and cast aside in favor again of the basics, yet those basics now performed with a deep joyful awareness of every angle, every moment, every fingertip.

Early in the year, renowned photographer Annie Leibovitz shoots an image of Lisa for *Condé Nast Sports for Women* on the sands of Ormond Beach, and in a simple kind of way, the photo says it all. It depicts as pure an athlete as surfing has seen: Lisa, stripped back to a surfer's basics of wetsuit and board, looks like she's beyond categories, beyond gender. Bad stuff just doesn't happen anymore. She draws the formidable Pam Burridge in heat after heat and makes her bring it to the table, and wins, and wins. She wins seven events of thirteen, a winning percentage nobody—woman or man—has matched in the history of the sport.

At the end of her diary for that year is a note from Veronica Kay: "You're my hero 'cos you made something out of nothing and did a lot more, instead of sitting on your ass feeling sorry for yourself waiting for the world to come to you."

PAGES 128–129: Erica always jumped onto me when I got out of the water.

This is a classic with Erica on Rochelle's shoulders.

Duranbah.
Australia. 1996.

4 . **T U R N I**

FROM LISA'S DIARY, APRIL 15, 1998:

I dreamt that I was buying ice cream for Erica in Japanese Restaurant and it cost $210.00. I tasted one and refused to buy them. I walked out and they said I would have a hard time with immigration.

Then I was surfing this beachbreak (I don't know where). Jeff was there shooting film.

I was paddling for this wave and Ross [Williams] pushed me into it. I just stood inside this huge barrel. I just kept going and going. It seemed like it was getting darker and darker. Then a glimpse of sunshine in the face showing me the way out. I thought for a second, I hope someone shot that. Guys were hooting going up the face. I saw like a thin part of the lip and just broke through, like going through a spider web. And then claimed it. I fell in slow motion thinking I was so happy that I didn't care how dumb I looked falling. I came in trying to tell this woman jogging by that I just got a 10 second barrel but she just kept running. Then there was Jeff and he said he shot the whole thing, but it was too dark. Then all the good feelings just disappeared.

Fear is the other side of love
Fear is the dread of love
Fear is the dread of losing what we have
and are. or letting go in order to
become what will be
We are afraid of love
Love demands all we are.

Lisa's handwriting does the same thing as her face: it changes. Sometimes sloping, aggressive, intelligent, swift. Sometimes rounded and upright and slower, not as engaged. Sometimes sparse and spidery and uncertain. When it's the first variety, it looks a lot like her mother's. The second is used to inscribe travel plans and diary dates. The third trails off pages, ends paragraphs, comes and goes almost without warning.

Lisa's run was over, though she didn't truly know it. She'd been planning on a 1998 retirement, in September, when Erica was due to start kindergarten; yet she was also tired, bone weary of the travel and the endless need to win, win, win. By the end of 1997 she'd won twenty of her

career twenty-one World Championship Tour victories and had begun an on-again, off-again relationship with Tom Servais, a *Surfer* magazine photographer. Tom, fifteen years older, was the right man at the right time for Lisa, who was somewhat on the rebound. While he was looking for a life partner, Lisa just found it fun; she could go out with Tom and do couples-type stuff with people like Rochelle and Bill Ballard, playing golf, drinking margaritas. When Lorraine met him, she looked at Lisa and said rather drily, "Him?"

"Mom, it's fine!" Lisa protested. "Yeah, I like him!"

"Okay . . ." said Lorraine.

Lisa kept seeing him until she arrived in Australia for the beginning of the '98 tour, where just before a heat, she was approached by young Aussie surfer Serena Brooke, who told her: "Look, everyone knows this but you, but Tom and I were just in Fiji, and now we're kinda together. . . . Okay, see you in the water!" Lisa lost the heat. Thereafter, wherever she went, there were Tom and Serena, and now *they* were hanging out with Rochelle and Bill; Lisa would go surfing, and there Tom would be shooting photos of Serena. It drove her quietly nuts. The

tour, once her sacred place of escape, had somehow become . . . tarnished.

Plus her back was tearing her up again. Maybe it was time to go home for a while.

In September, as she'd intended, Lisa took Erica back to Ormond Beach and did that most

domestic of tasks: enrolled her daughter in school. If she'd thought the coming year would be settled and domestic, that thought was soon eroded. In 1999 she began a series of trips on Quiksilver's new Crossing project, a seemingly endless voyage around the world on the former Indonesian surf-exploration vessel *Indies Trader 1,* crewed by the company's top pros and

TOP, LEFT TO RIGHT: Unloading the boat in Tavarua, Fiji.
Posing on a black-sand beach in Tahiti.
First all-girls Crossing trip, in Tahiti.

ABOVE: The Crossing was my rescue boat, my knight in shining armor.
I put everything on hold and sailed off.

Trying to
emulate
my hero.
Tom Curren.
Crossing trip.
Tahiti.

their guests. She would be with Veronica and Megan and the rest of the Roxy stars, Hornbaker would be there, they would spend two weeks at a time roaming the open ocean from island to atoll, and the blue sea and sky leaked through Lisa's senses. After one trip, she wrote, "I love the silence it brings to me. I hope to get back to that silence. I hate being alone. And I love being alone."

She was torn between weariness and wanderlust, between home comforts and the lure of the world.

Here is one thing she did love about life back in Florida: surfing. Lisa returned to the waves of her childhood armed with the skills of an unassailable champion and found she truly loved those little waves, on the beautiful, unusual days when a good swell would meet an offshore wind and New Smyrna or Ponce Inlet would begin to look like France, with head-high and bigger barrels peeling off sandbars everywhere. There'd be days, sure, when it would be deadly boring mush, and she'd begin to wish for the Hawaiian season to come around, or for another Crossing trip. But there'd be other days, days of swell and currents, and Shea and Cory Lopez would come over, and the boys would be competitive and a little crazy with Lisa, because she'd be on fire. Lisa would get back to what she'd cherished on tour: that feeling of being with her peers, just one of the boys, and blowing their minds with her pure lines, her fingertip control, and perfect style. She'd have her best board, a new Merrick, and a backup board, and

Florida free surf.

the boys would be watching and saying to her: "What the *hell* are you doing here! What are you *on!*"

Those good days always seemed sunny and warm, and Lisa would drive her car down onto the beach, and the local kids would hang around because they'd know she had food, and they'd want to check out her boards—looking up to her, but in a natural, unforced way, the way surf kids everywhere look up to the best surfer at their beach. The essence of the surfing family, as it plays out, at surf spots everywhere from Ormond Beach to Waikiki. It was *sooo* laid-back. It was laid-back to a point where it could feel as if you were disappearing—falling off the face of the earth, and not even realizing it.

For Christmas in 1999 the Raymonds came to visit Lisa. Both Bruce and Janice wanted to see where their amazing protégée had grown up, and how she was handling herself at home these days. Arguments over money were by now in the past, as was Mike Kingsbury; now Lisa was represented by the Los Angeles–based Jane Kachmer and, ironically, being paid nearly twice as much as when she'd been winning world titles.

Still, she was spending it just as fast: mortgages on her home and an investment property, cameras, computer gear—along with photography, Lisa always had a thing for electronic gadgetry. Bruce advised her to find ways to cut back.

One afternoon Lisa collared Janice and took her to a back room, telling her to come and look out the window at this, *look*. What? asked Janice.

"The gardener! Look at his legs," Lisa almost whispered.

Janice loved this! Paul Osbaldiston was a motocross-riding landscape gardener, originally from New Zealand and still with plenty of antipodean accent about him, and Janice noted with interest that he did indeed have nice legs.

Put yourself out there, Janice urged, Come on, you need a bloke. But I've tried, Lisa countered. He won't bite. Then ask him out! And Lisa did.

Meeting Paul freed her up—in one way, at least. She finally divorced Renato. On June 23, 2000, in fact, through a lawyer named Anne Marie McDonald, paying $750 for the official "dissolution of marriage."

Paul. Master
BBQ chef.

Tahiti, 2000.

ONE DOOR CLOSES, ANOTHER OPENS

In March 2000, feeling the competitive energy rising in her, uncomfortable with the notion that she was sliding from the world's sight, sensing the need to make some sort of statement, Lisa applied for and was granted the ASP tour's injury wild card. She came back to the world tour at the Billabong Pro event on Australia's Gold Coast, and immediately ran second to Layne Beachley.

Now Layne was the champ, and she didn't let Lisa forget it. Lisa didn't. The months went by as she rebuilt her heat skills: a ninth at Bells Beach, a strong third at Jeffreys Bay. In Europe, she began finding that space again, that familiar place where she could shut everyone out, and she did just that: hid under a hooded sweatshirt with headphones and sunglasses, drove her own car, cleared an opening for herself. In the

Mason. the water baby.

final of the last big French event, at Anglet, she turned the tables on Beachley, winning easily. Her ranking jumped to third, within striking distance of a fifth title.

Then she found out she was pregnant.

"I had to tell Quiksilver," Lisa recalls. "It's the worst thing you can tell your sponsor: I'm *pregnant*." She's grinning at the memory, her eyes glinting a little wickedly. Again, there's that flash of her strength, her solidity—perhaps it's something parenthood has given her.

Actually, she told Rochelle first, crying at the time, not for the child to come but for what she knew in her heart she was walking away from. Yet she was okay with it, because in her heart she wanted a child—a boy. As did Erica. Every day Erica would say it four hundred times: "I want a little brother! I want a little brother! I want a little brother!" No getting away from it.

This time, pregnancy came on strong. It was as if her body had spoken, saying, "I remember this!" and swung into the process without any fooling around. She was sick almost straightaway, tired easily, and lost her appetite for surfing. She decided to relax; she walked her dog, Sam, over the Ormond Beach connecting bridge to the surf side each day, swam, and lay on the beach until her skin was almost black. Lisa wasn't sure if Paul really wanted any part of it, but when they went for an ultrasound checkup and the fetus could be seen with one arm turned up toward the face, Paul said, "Yep, pretty sure it's a boy, he's holding a beer!" Late in the pregnancy, the doctors decided to induce the birth. Something went wrong, or not quite right; Lisa can't quite recall, but she thinks some fluid leaked into the baby's lungs. Labor came on in a rush, with enormous pain, and Lisa felt like she was dying, being stabbed in the lower back, screaming with it, the opposite of Erica's arrival. The doctors gave her something to ease the pain, and she calmed down. Paul was there, with a couple of buddies outside, and they mixed up a pitcher of martinis in a kind of pre-birth celebration.

Thus came Mason, her little boy, entering the world at 8:24 P.M. on June 4, 2001, and Lisa again was struck by it all: how amazing it is that you have this little thing inside of you, your body wrestling with it for months, and the next thing you know, it's looking at you.

History repeats itself in a person's life, but never in quite the same way. With Mason, maybe, Lisa crossed another line in the sand, began another initiation. That win at Anglet—her last-ever tour victory—pushed her to an eventual fifth in the world in 2000, and she never ranked higher than fifteenth again. "I had a ridiculous number of chances to do it," she says of her comeback that wasn't. "And I just couldn't do it. It was getting to the point where it woulda been way more damaging to keep trying. . . . People at Roxy were saying, 'We don't want you to go out there and kill yourself, throw yourself at the mercy of everyone and look like this person struggling to come back.'

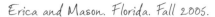
Erica and Mason. Florida. Fall 2005.

the reunion with her tour buddies, paid only cursory attention. Paul had no connection with the surfing world, and Lisa was surprised to find him upset, threatened by its place in her life beyond Ormond Beach. It disturbed her to think the two—Paul and surfing—might not be able to coexist. She surfed in the event and lost a close but decisive heat to Layne, finishing effectively last.

Later she took on one of the classic ex–world champ tour tasks, event direction, at the Roxy Pro-Am on Phillip Island, Australia. In the plane on the way home she wrote, "Flying these days makes me go insane. I have no nails left and my ears are sore from headphones. . . . I miss my mom, my babies, my kitchen. Wish I could sleep. . . .

"When I come home from a trip it's sometimes like I've been deflated like, I don't know, just it's not the same, I have to become a whole different person. There [are] bills to pay, kids to bathe, a relationship to hold together. When I am out there doing what I do I get put on a pedestal in a way, then I just feel so unappreciated when I return home. I wish he could be different. I love way more than I get loved. Maybe I choose all the wrong ones. There's always something missing."

By early 2005, Lisa was feeling more and more stranded. She wasn't going back to the tour. She was sliding further down into anonymity. So many things were attaching her to this half-chosen life: a big new mortgage on a big new house she and Paul had bought on the

"And I wasn't struggling to come back. I was really happy with what I'd done. But I think I felt I had to try."

Roxy took off some of the heat, cutting her salary in half and freeing her from any responsibility, with a bonus clause for any tasks she did perform. Lisa drifted, somewhere between the old life, the traveling circus, and this new life she'd half-selected for herself back home in Ormond Beach. In March 2003, she traveled with Paul and Mason and Erica to Queensland, Australia, for the first Roxy-backed event of the ASP year. The trip was not a big success. Paul's parents came over from New Zealand to meet their grandson; Lisa, busy with the event and

When I go back to Florida, I could take off the Lisa Andersen suit and go somewhere — I don't know where.

waterway; Paul himself; Lorraine; Mason. Yet there was so much she couldn't do! She confided in the Raymonds, Randy Hild, and others. "I had people in my life telling me to move to California, your career could be that much bigger, there's that much more you can do when you're in the public eye and more in the surf industry," she says. "Which I knew to be true. But I was obligated, you know, and it wasn't on the list that I could just walk away and do that.

"I dunno. It freaks me out," Lisa adds. "I still think about it all the time. I'm not the kind of person who'd enjoy fame at that level. I don't want to be a 'celebrity.' But . . . I'd just basically given it up without even trying. Let all the possibilities go."

As she tells her stories on fall afternoons in the house at Huntington, late sunlight streaming through the windows, Lisa comes back around again to this sense of something missing, how it drives her at times. "It's that thing about wanting something you can't have, then when you get it you don't want it," she says.

Lisa throws back her head—her eyes are clouded over, thinking. She's inches away from something, some revelation. She looks down, and the moment passes. "Ahh," she says quietly, "I dunno what I'm saying." But she does.

In June, she makes up her mind, makes one of her Decisions.

The Roxy job, global brand ambassador, is there for her if she chooses. She still has time, she's still young, she can make something of herself. She wants something she *can* have. She tells Paul it's over, leaves him in the big new house on the waterway, packs what she can, leaves what she can't. Six weeks later she's gone.

ORMOND BEACH, SEPTEMBER 2005:

Here again, now, on a humid Florida weekend, in the house of the aunts' yard sale. This is where Lisa ran to with Erica and Mason, after leaving Paul on the waterway.

The house is half empty, half full with bits and pieces of their lives. There are fourteen surfboards in the laundry room, mostly beautiful high-performance Al Merricks, though a couple are trophy boards, including one shaped by the legendary Australian world champion Mark Richards. There are seven large snap-shut plastic boxes full of tour memories: winning-event jerseys, classic early Roxy boardshorts,

FEAR-LESS-NESS

Another Tahiti boat trip: lots of left-handers there.

old wetsuits, competition judging sheets, notes she'd written to herself.

In her office there are photo albums piled on photo albums, but they have little to do with surfing. They're full of Lisa's photos: her friends, her lovers, her family, and her children, extraordinary photos of Erica and of Mason, at every age, in every mood, alone and with each other.

Somewhere in the concertina folders of office papers is an invoice dated August 7, 2003, from Carl W. Lentz, a Daytona Beach plastic surgeon, for breast-implant surgery. Later, Lisa doesn't blink when asked about this; instead she laughs cheerily, and a bit wickedly. "Yeah, I wasn't happy with how they looked," she says. "After two kids, are you kidding me? Here they were just about hanging down into my cereal at breakfast. I wanted to feel good about myself again, and I'd never really been too happy with that part of me. . . . It was about becoming a sexy person again."

It's strange, this looking through a house half-deserted by its owner. Fortunately, Lorraine is here, doing some cleaning up after the sale, and sighing at all the stuff Lisa still has to drag across the continent to Huntington. And here now at the front door is Nicole, a close friend of Lisa's from the Seabreeze Senior High days, to have a coffee and talk.

Nicole Currey moved to Ormond Beach from Miami in 1982, around the same time as the Andersens came south from Fork Union. This, Nicole thinks, is how she and Lisa got to be friends, despite a two-year age gap. "We were just good girls, having fun," she says. At thirty-eight, Nicole is attractive, friendly, easygoing—not totally unlike her superstar friend, in fact—and eager to offer a positive take on Lisa: "Lisa's a photographer, she's a writer, she's very artistic." In between the praise, she tells more of the story.

They hung out at the old Ormond Beach pier, north of town—not far from Nicole's house. Nicole could drive down and pick up Lisa from the house on Bosarvey Drive on the way to school. "*When* we went to school," she adds. "Depending on what was going on—how the beach was." Nicole didn't surf, but she says she could pick Lisa in the water by her style and aggression. "That's how she got that name, Trouble. There were no other girls in the water." She says they had in fact heard of Frieda Zamba, but Flagler Beach, twenty miles north, might as well have been on another planet.

What was life like at the Andersen house? Nicole pauses. "Lisa's kids have a great life," she says. "She makes a great home for them. There's lots of light, greenness. It's decorated. This was not like her childhood home. It was minimal. There wasn't anything—no feeling. None of what you expect in a family. If we made a snack, it was cleaned up instantly. And quiet. Never any sound. It wasn't somewhere we hung out, that's for sure."

After May 1985, Nicole did not see or hear from her friend until late 1994, at the Surf Expo trade show in Orlando, when she saw a small girl being carried on the shoulders of a dark-haired man and instantly recognized Lisa's face. "That's Erica!" she thought and, after introducing herself to Renato, followed them back to the Quiksilver stand, where Lisa and Kelly Slater were sitting in front of a crowd signing autographs. "I think it was right then I realized how far she'd come."

Nicole works at these surfing trade shows, helping with hospitality and organization. Once again you wonder, What else has become of Lisa's other schoolmates? Surfing back then was cool enough, but nobody was thinking about it as a big career. Might a less driven Lisa, a less anguished and alienated girl, have lived a life like Nicole's, closer to home?

For her part, Nicole sees Lisa now as "a warrior," someone who took on the world on her own terms and earned what she's gained.

"Lisa takes big steps," she says seriously. "She takes real big steps. She's very brave. . . . She works at relationships, but she'll walk away if she has to.

"It's a natural thing for her now, going to Huntington. She's gone back to where she first started."

Fiji. 2005.

5. MOVING

EARLY SPRING 2006, NOW, ON A FOGGY SORT OF DAY, AROUND NOON, AND LISA IS ALONE IN THE HOUSE IN HUNTINGTON, MOPPING THE FLOOR. Much of the stuff from the Ormond Beach house has now been moved to Huntington Beach. Her garage is full of it: surfboards, trophies, toys. Some of it has made it into the house: flat-screen TV; various trophies, including the massive 1997 World Championship cup, a thing the size of a Halloween pumpkin; an aerial photo of Ponce Inlet looking up toward Daytona and Ormond.

"It was sooo dirty—I'd never had a chance to do this," she says as she mops, though the floor had never seemed dirty before.

She's occupying herself, partly to quiet her nerves. Lisa is still on edge after the past week, which she spent mostly in Ormond Beach, in family court over Mason. Paul, she says, has been increasingly stubborn about it. Did she expect this? "Totally," she says. "I mean, whether or not he's a good dad, that's not in question."

She flops onto the giant beanbag and talks about it for a while.

Mason is a real absence in this house. The current arrangement is for him to go back and forth between Florida and California until at least April. Sometime in there, they'll all go back to court and a ruling will be made on custody. Amazingly, Paul's attorney, Horace Smith, is the same lawyer who represented John Andersen against Lorraine in the 1980s.

"Paul's told people he wants to destroy me financially," she says seriously. "You know, I don't think so. I don't want to destroy *him*. He's got to be Mason's father." She seems oddly oblivious to the idea that her actions might somehow be playing a part in his pain and anger . . . or maybe she feels the waterway house makes up for it all. "He should be happy," she says. "He has a rental near the beach—he could sell it and have a lot of money on top of that house."

Eventually she calms down enough to talk about other things—life around Huntington, and a short-lived romance, which she's sure makes no sense at all. "There's sooo many obstacles," she says, "I wasn't looking for this to come along.

"So now you know it all," she finishes with a flourish. "Maybe we should do a soap opera."

"The Many Lives and Loves of Lisa. The Perilous Life of Miss Lisa Andersen."

"I'm a sucker for romance," she says, beginning to make two huge sandwiches of pastrami, turkey, and provolone for lunch. "It feels so great to have someone treat you well."

The change of subject lifts her mood, and she takes some time to explain about the tiny F E A R L E S S N E S S plaque she wears around her neck. It was given to her by actress Mariska Hargitay, of *Law and Order: SVU* fame, and is intended to symbolize the battle against child sexual abuse, and the great character quality required to rise above such abuse and live as you might choose. Perhaps for Lisa, it symbolizes other battles, too, ones she also intends to win. "I want to be on the board [of Quiksilver] one day," she says. "It might take a long time. Ten,

I'm really a fish.

twenty years, who knows? I told my mom and she said, 'Well, you told me you wanted to be world champion one day, too.'"

Where are they, all the ones who've passed through Lisa's life? Ray Ferrantelli pursued her on and off through the 1980s, telling one of her sponsors she owed him money, then vanished. Two years ago Lisa walked into a bank in Ormond Beach, carrying Mason, looked across the lobby, and saw Ray at one of the teller windows. She is sure it was him. A shadow of old fear drove her out of the bank. She hasn't seen him since.

Craig Comen is living in northern California, teaching yoga and running kayak tours. He recently married a Chilean girl; they have a house in her homeland, at a surf spot called Punta Lobos. Tom Servais is no longer with Serena Brooke; he recently published a beautiful big book of his photographs and made sure Lisa got a copy.

Wendy Botha lives on the Gold Coast in Queensland, Australia, runs a small business with her husband, Brent, and owns four boards, though she's more likely to steal her twelve-year-old daughter Jessica's little round-nose for a surf. She still wrestles with how the great girls' boom occurred—not so much about the fact that she missed it, but why it happened when it did. She has no connection with the surf industry. Her eyes are as blue and friendly as ever.

Renato is around, always contactable, though as he says, "If we've had a thousand phone conversations since the separation, I've made nine hundred and fifty of 'em." Of Lisa's men, Renato is the only one who made friends with John Andersen, yet the friendship hasn't denied him this insight on behalf of the rest: "Perhaps in all of us there was a little bit of a father figure. Perhaps because the one who should have looked after her at the start fucked up."

Dave Parmenter spent one or two lonely years after Lisa left him, surfing and making boards for a select Central Coast crew before moving to Makaha, on Oahu's West Side—Makaha, home to great watermen and waterwomen from the days before even Duke Kahanamoku. There he encountered the extraordinary Rell Sunn and fell utterly for the woman who above all others represented the power of femininity and ocean commingled. Rell surfed, she canoed, she ran competitions for the displaced West Side kids, she could fill a fish bag with a hand spear, at her home there was a bath-tub filled with ukuleles for anyone and everyone to play. She and Dave were married within a year. But Rell had breast cancer, a disease even the waterwoman couldn't shake, and in January 1998, after nursing her all the way through it, he laid her to rest.

Lisa wrote to him to tell him how sorry she was—her first attempt to

CLOCKWISE FROM TOP:

My heroes — Shane, Conan, Rob, and Ross, Portugal, 1997.

My best pal, Pat, Portugal, 1997.

Australia Roxy shoot.

Andy Irons, J-Bay. He always had a crush on me.

CLOCKWISE FROM TOP:
Kealia, V.K., Alalo,
and me.
Kalani, Robb and me.
Traveling through
Japan.
Megan Abubo's pad.
Hawaii.

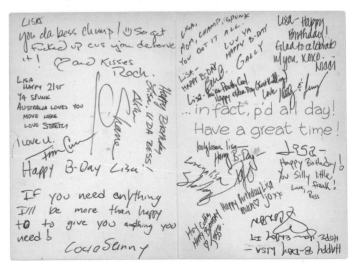

Fiji. 1996.

contact Dave since 1994, when she'd asked him to make her a board. Then he'd cut her off with a terse "I'm not a fan." But the time with Rell had changed him. He wrote back in return, saying, among other things, "I spent the day with Hornbaker the other day, and he told me that you've changed a lot, and are taking care of your mom. If that's true, then I'm proud of you . . . more proud than I could ever be over anything you've accomplished with your surfing.

"I can't believe it's been ten years. We've both taken such different paths, but I only have forgiveness in my heart, and wish for you the best in life. If you have your health and surfing, you have everything—never forget that! Aloha, Dave."

Now, in 2006, Parmenter has been back in touch again. Lisa speaks of this like somebody who's won some sort of prize. They exchanged e-mails; Dave was on California's Central Coast at the time, and suggested she call. "Don't know if I'm quite ready for that," she says wryly, with a smile. She can't really remember his face. She's scared to talk to him, scared to see him. What would it be like, revisiting that decision? She doesn't know.

She misses the tour and the tour misses her.

MARCH 8, 2006: LISA'S BIRTHDAY. She's in a

bar in Laguna Beach, California. It's late but not too late; she's buzzed but not too buzzed. She

decides to call Rochelle, pops the number up, and presses DIAL. The phone rings in Rochy's pocket seventy-five hundred miles away, upstairs in the Rainbow Bay Surf Club in Coolangatta, Australia, Quiksilver and Roxy Pro headquarters for the week, where all the surfers are gathered having a quiet afternoon beer. It's the first big pro event of the year. "Happy birthday!" sings Rochelle, accusing Lisa of being drunk, then hands the phone to the surfer standing next to her. It's Matt Hoy, Hoyo, who yells a delighted Australian obscenity at his once-upon-a-time seductress, and hands the phone on to the surfer next to him, Occy, Mark Occhilupo, the only surfer now on tour to predate Lisa's time. Occ is equally delighted, talks for a minute, then hands the phone on . . . and Rochelle's phone does a circuit of the room in Coolangatta while Lisa stands outside the

Birthday card from close pals.

Goofing with
Rochelle and
Chelsea.

bar in Laguna, half drunk, listening to all the voices from an ocean away, the eternal runaways in their traveling circus, which has now traveled on. Or which she's now left behind. Or a bit of both.

John Andersen didn't return any of the many phone calls I made to him during the course of researching and writing this book. He now lives in Orlando, Florida, with his third wife.

Lorraine Lemelin looks at her prodigal daughter now and is happy for her. "I just want her to be financially secure in her life, her and the children," says Lorraine decisively. "That's the main thing. I think now where she's heading in her life she's gonna be just fine. Hopefully one day in her life she'll find that one person who really cares about her, not somebody who wants to use her. . . . She'll find time to find someone for herself, who really deserves her."

Yet Lorraine still doesn't understand exactly what Lisa gains from surfing. She knows Lisa finds it exhilarating, that people have told her Lisa in the water is the happiest person in the world, that Lisa will come in from surfing and always have something good to say about it.

Lorraine thinks about how to relate to it. "Dancing," she says at last, quite suddenly. "I love to dance. I took dancing lessons for about fifteen years from my aunt, she had a dancing school. I started when I was about five years old, did 'Dance of the Wooden Soldiers'. . . . I just love to dance! I love it, I love it. And that's

what upsets me about being deaf and not being able to hear music. It's not just the music, it's being able to dance. I keep the tempo but I have no idea what the song is. I can understand how surfing might compare with that."

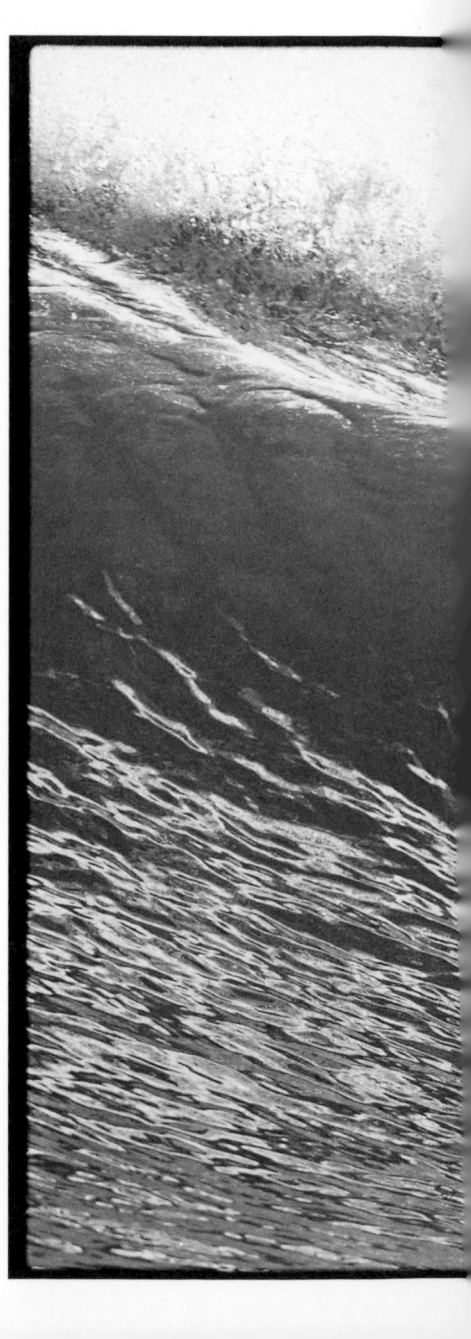

Indo. 2006.

LISA, AUGUST 2006: A YEAR NOW AFTER LISA PRESENTED HER BUSINESS CARD IN THE QUIKSILVER OFFICE AT HUNTINGTON BEACH.

She's moved out of the halfway house her employer had rented for her and into a smaller, more open house of her choice, with a garden, a block or two away. Soon Mason and Erica will both be back with her—Mason from half a summer at Paul's in Florida, Erica from a couple of weeks with Renato—and she's happy they'll be

coming here. Mason's artwork is already hanging on a wall. "There's more light here, you know?" she says. "More space around the house."

She's still single, though there's a boy up around Malibu, where she's been hanging out with Laird Hamilton and Gabrielle Reece, recovering from shoulder surgery, and learning to paddle-surf, Nalu-style, standing and using the long paddle. She's thirty-seven years old.

She makes coffee, lolls on a couch, watches the surf movie playing on the flat-screen TV. The movie is called *Shimmer*, and it is something you couldn't have imagined in 1985: a straight-up high-quality surf action feature full of no one but girls surfing—not ironically, not "like girls," but like whoever they happen to be.

Here and there, Lisa comes into the frame. The shots are from July 2005, the trip Megan Abubo had mentioned. Lisa's back had kept her from surfing for seven days; on the eighth, she paddled out and rode the best two waves of the trip. The rides come into frame now: Lisa turning off the wave base with power yet with that half-smiling attentiveness, feeling her way through each turn with ease.

"I was at one of the trial screenings," she chortles, "and this young guy's like 'Wow, she's pretty good! How old is she?'"

The next morning, not too early, she will take the freeway north and get on Highway 101 toward Malibu for a day of paddling, surfing, chilling. With the kids coming home, it might be her last chance for a while.

What's changed in Lisa is hard to tell, but something's changed. As she talks about her plans, it somehow evokes a memory of the words she'd spoken a year before in the Quiksilver office: "You know, I was always looking for the good." Maybe it's this simple: somehow, in her long year of transition, twenty-one years after she'd first run away, Lisa's found the good she was looking for—or enough of it for now, at least. Enough fearlessness to last awhile. And she isn't turning back.

Fearlessness.

PHOTOGRAPHY CREDITS

AUTHOR BIOGRAPHIES

NICK CARROLL is a former editor of *Surfing* magazine and the author of *The Next Wave.* He lives in Australia.

LISA ANDERSEN is the four-time world champion of surfing. She lives in southern California with her daughter, Erica, and son, Mason.

ACKNOWLEDGMENTS

As is always the case with these kind of lists, I am certain to miss lots of people who have been and remain key parts of my life. Let me get it out of the way and apologize now. You and I both know who you are.

That said, let me thank my Mom, Dad, Duane and Scott, my extended family, and my children Erica and Mason. I love you all and wouldn't be the person I am without each of you.

Bruce and Janice Raymond (and Ben and Nick) are truly my second family. Thanks so much for everything you've done with and for me.

My manager, Mitch Varnes, and my biography's author, Nick Carroll, for their dedication, passion, and prodding in seeing *Fearlessness* from inception to publication.

And an especially heartfelt thank-you to those who have been such influences in my life and with this book: Renato Hickel, Paul Osbaldiston, Dave Parmenter, Craig Comen, Nicole Carrey, Ian Cairns, Pierre Agnes, Rob Rowland-Smith, Andrew Murphy, Jane Kachner, Jeff Hornbaker, Tom Servais, Steve Sherman, Joli, Art Brewer, Al Merrick, Xanadu, John Carper, Bob Hurley, Butch Barr, Fernando Aguerre, Maritxu Darragrand, Bob McKnight, Randy Hild, Bernard Mariette, Veronica Kay, Tom Carroll, Wendy Botha, Sarah Malarkey, and Tim Shannon.

To everyone at Quiksilver, Roxy, Reef, Dakine, and Channel Islands, thank you.

—LA